Good Faith Hunting

Good Faith Hunting

How Baby Boomers Helped Recapture a Biblical View of Faith

HENRY STEWART

With a Foreword by Michael S. Moore

WIPF & STOCK · Eugene, Oregon

GOOD FAITH HUNTING
How Baby Boomers Helped Recapture a Biblical View of Faith

Wipf & Stock
An Imprint of Wipf and Stock Publishers
199 W. 8th Ave., Suite 3
Eugene, OR 97401
www.wipfandstock.com

ISBN 13: 98-1-62032-219-2

Manufactured in the U.S.A.

For my wife Karen
she is a constant inspiration to me

Contents

List of Illustrations

Foreword

It had already been a long day, but Henry wanted me to go with him to visit the midweek service of the predominantly Iraqi congregation meeting that evening near the center of downtown Amman, Jordan. So we hailed a cab outside the hotel and soon joined up with our Arabic-speaking brothers and sisters for what we naively imagined to be a one hour service or so. After a couple of hours, though, the singing began to wind down a bit and one of the pastors stood up to introduce "our American guests," thereby proffering us the opportunity to hand over to them the gift we had brought over from the States—a brand new, state-of-the-art, video projector. Pulling it from the bag, we saw one of the worship leaders jump down from the makeshift stage in the corner of the room and start hugging us. Unable to respond to him in his native tongue, Henry and I just smiled and beamed and drank it all in.

Invited for tea and biscuits afterwards, we meekly protested that we were too tired to stay, but our hosts would have none of *that*. So, not only did we drink tea with our new friends for another hour or so, we also listened to their stories—some joyous, some routine, some comical, some heartbreaking. Most of the members of this predominantly male congregation, you see, were recent Iraqi refugees forced to flee their families as multinational forces invaded their country. Many didn't know if they were ever going to see their loved ones again, and they desperately wanted someone to pray with them about it. So Henry and I listened and prayed and drank tea with these members of the Body at this holy moment. It was an unforgettable experience.

Riding back to the hotel in the cab, I still remember the excitement in Henry's voice as he helped us process what we'd just experienced. How often do two white boys born in the suburbs of the Virginia Tidewater region get to do what we'd just done?

The book you're about to read is designed to help you process what you're experiencing, particularly if you're part of the growing nation of disciples which finds itself increasingly fed up with the "counterfeit community" and "club Christianity" now masquerading as the Body of Christ in North America.

So put the kettle on, put your legs up, and enjoy the ride back to the hotel . . .

Michael S. Moore
Director, Arizona Research Center for the Ancient Near East
Faculty Associate, Arizona State University, Fuller Theological Seminary
Author of *The Balaam Traditions* (1990), *Faith Under Pressure* (2003), and *WealthWatch* (2011)

Preface

For the past twenty years or so, church leaders in the United States and other western nations have been desperately trying to maintain the organizations they used to know well. Those leaders who are honest with themselves recognize that they have not been able to slow down or reverse the attendance losses. The losses are much greater than can be explained by the simplistic canard, "Young people don't like church." Societal interest in transcendence and spirituality is increasing, so why are people of all ages avoiding church? Contrary to popular opinion, it's not only young people avoiding our sanctuaries. The losses are particularly noticeable in the baby boomer generation, many of whom grew up with at least some exposure to faith and church.

I too am concerned about this present reality and the future of churches in America, so I dug further into the underlying causes and possible responses during my DMin studies at George Fox University. Much of the basic research for this book comes from my doctoral dissertation exploring baby boomers and faith journeys. In the dissertation, I concluded that baby boomers had shifted to a more postmodern way of thinking much earlier than commonly believed and therefore, process the world more similar to their children rather than their parents. This in turn, carries heavy impact on church attendance. My research findings propelled me to investigate boomer culture and boomers' unique faith journeys, looking for connections to their desire, or lack of desire to take their place on a pew. I wasn't satisfied with data analysis, but rather, I wanted to look into people's eyes and hear their stories.

A number of people generously contributed their time for stories of journeys, interviews, or discussions. These conversations kept me focused on the human capacity and possibilities for connecting with God. They include Bill Burden, Gary Fluharty, Mary Frank, Lorelei Hillman, Norman Johnson, Crystal Miller, Troy Miller, Rick Palmer, Joe Powers,

John Rae, Betsy Shirey, Sharon Schaefer, and others who wish to remain anonymous.

Dr. Donna K. Wallace, a *New York Times* bestselling author, book architect, and fellow George Fox Seminary alum, helped rescue this book project when it desperately needed assistance to make it into print. Her premier sense of flow and storytelling pulled me out of blind alleys of my own construction and myopia.

I want to make special mention of Dr. Michael S. Moore, a First (Old) Testament scholar, Semitic language expert, and a good friend. He opened my eyes to the richness and depth of the wilderness accounts and the entirety of the *Tanakh,* the Hebrew Bible. He is one of those people who prod the Christian Church to reclaim the full Gospel, which starts at Creation rather than coming into existence *ex nihilo,* out of nothing, at the birth of Jesus Christ. Dr. Moore's insightful analysis of the Hebrew people's journey out of Egypt helped me connect their story with the sojourns of the Iraqi refugees we met in Amman. On the way back to the hotel I realized how God is with all who seek faith across the entirety of human history. Like the refugees, baby boomers follow in the footsteps of the slaves' flight out of Egypt with doubts, uncertainties, and trials.

When our own journey is lonely or confusing and we fear that Christ has abandoned us, hungry and thirsty in the trackless wilderness, the Apostle Paul reminds us of our eternal hope:

> I'm absolutely convinced that nothing—nothing living or dead, angelic or demonic, today or tomorrow, high or low, thinkable or unthinkable—absolutely *nothing* can get between us and God's love because of the way that Jesus our Master has embraced us. (Rom 8:38–39 MSG)

Introduction

My faith in Christ is central to my life. My conversion from a pessimistic atheist lost in a world I didn't understand, to an optimistic believer in a universe created and sustained by a loving God is crucial to me. But following Christ does not mean following His followers. Christ is infinitely more important than Christianity and always will be, no matter what Christianity is, has been, or might become.

—Anne Rice,
"Important Information about Anne's Decision."

One Friday morning in the late 1990s I drove to my engineering job by my normal route, listening to country music on the radio and not thinking much about my job. I got out of my old pickup truck, walked into the building and sat down at my desk, then got up to get a cup of coffee. So far, it was a normal sunny day in Mesa, Arizona. After I got my coffee, I sat down to start the day's work. An hour later, my boss came by and asked to see me in his office. Shortly thereafter, I walked down to his office, unconcerned about what we might discuss.

The moment I walked in, I realized nothing was normal when I saw both my boss and the head of human resources. They dropped a bombshell on me—I had three months to find a new job before mine vanished.

I guess I should have been thankful that I was not terminated on the spot, but thanksgiving was not on my mind as I walked out of the office in a daze. I was not mad, just stunned. In previous positions, I had always been an excellent engineer and a top performer. The company I worked for had recruited me to help them enter a new product area. However, for the last few months nothing seemed to work right. People working for me resigned, peers in the company no longer trusted my judgment, and the management was unhappy with my lack of progress in penetrating the new market.

That night I planned to attend a training class at a local church. Unsure if I wanted to go after such a punch to my gut, I went anyway. The leader asked each of us to introduce ourselves and share some of our journey with the group. When my turn came, I spoke of how I had felt like Jonah, running from God or at least trying to avoid God for many years. God called Jonah to go to Nineveh, yet Jonah ran away as fast as possible toward Tarshish, which was at the opposite end of the known world (Jonah 1:1–3). I ran like Jonah, and my Tarshish was California, the opposite coast from where I had started. I did not share anything about what had happened earlier that day.

The leader looked at me and asked, "Is Mesa your Ninevah?" He was asking me if Christ called me to serve in Mesa. I looked back at him in shock barely stammering out, "I don't know." All my negative thoughts I wanted hidden kept coming to the surface. Could my family and I stay in Mesa? Why had I not been able to perform better? How was I going to tell my wife that I was out of a job? How could I support my family and keep a roof over their heads? What worth did I have as a man if I was not the provider? My inability to solve the problems destroyed my sense of self-worth. I was an engineer, after all, and should be able to solve any problem. I did not expect such a major paradigm shift and I ended up lost at sea without a rudder or anchor.

Since then, I've speculated that God was tired of whispering in my ear, and decided to use a "2x4" of a job loss to get my attention. I would not have re-arranged my locus of meaning otherwise. I would have remained happy with leaving Christ on the shelf as "fire insurance" since I believed there was no point in bothering him with the little stuff. I could handle the details myself.

Was that chapter of my life as dramatic as Jonah being puked up on shore after spending three days in the gut of a giant fish? Perhaps not, but Jonah's journey remains a powerful metaphor for the experiences God had in mind for my future. I would not have encountered so many new friends on my voyage of exploration had I not been brought to my knees by Christ. I would have missed listening to new friends in other countries as they shared accounts of being tortured for following Christ. I would have missed visiting people in prison. I would have missed sharing tears, hearing wisdom and seeing strength in people as they faced death. I would have missed celebrating great triumphs in life. I would have missed people reaching out to me when I needed help. I would have missed coming face-to-face with Christ, invited by someone who planned to defraud me. *Yet none of these intense and profound experiences happened within a church sanctuary or within a church building.*

In 1952, I was born into the baby boomer generation. Boomers, born between 1946 and 1964, are feeling the impact of similar traumatic events like mine such as illnesses, job losses, the deaths of friends and family members, changes in relationships, empty nesting, and the results of earlier decisions that have lifetime effects. We are members of a unique transition generation undergoing redefinitions of the basic nature of knowledge and the ways in which we communicate truth. The changes in boomer lives are inevitable with age and experiences coupled with cataclysmic societal changes. Baby boomers have been forced to re-examine their primary sources of meaning, and this includes their faith.

This cusp generation also set the tone, economics, worship styles, and the political agenda for the United States and indeed much of the western world from the 1960s until the current time. Now baby boomers are looking backward and forward simultaneously, asking if what they did with their life was worth the effort, and what they should spend the rest of their life doing. Many are deeply questioning the definitions of faith, worship, and church as they transition into different phases of their lives. Boomers are asking why they are stuck journeying through an apparent wilderness without visible signposts, sound, water, or the smell of fresh new life for what seems to them an eternity. Together with younger generations, boomers are on a similar quest. In the midst of *Good Faith Hunting*, many are afraid they have lost the map.

Does belief really remain constant over a lifetime? How does it morph and flower when it strikes events headlong? If a person changes some aspect of his or her life and says, "I was wrong," does that not imply one's faith or understanding of faith changed? When someone leaves a church or stops attending church, has he changed, has she left Christian faith, or is something else occurring?

Several years ago, baby boomer author Anne Rice made headlines when she "quit Christianity," announcing it on her Facebook page.

Many media commentators stated, or suggested, that she was moving from a belief in Christ into agnosticism or atheism.[1] Is Anne Rice no longer a follower of Christ wandering in a wilderness, or has she merely rejected specific denominational or doctrinal stances? How can someone who "abandoned" Christian faith make such a deep confession of belief, "*Following Christ does not mean following his followers. Christ is infinitely more important than Christianity and always will be.*"[2] Her powerful statement shows how deeply she accepts being a follower of Christ.

The institution of the western Christian church is in trouble. Attendance is rapidly declining, and I believe the available statistics do not reveal the magnitude of the loss. Many church leaders ignore the problem, attempting to mask the losses with misleading or incomplete data. George Barna writes, "After nearly two decades of studying Christian churches in America, I'm convinced that the typical church as we know it today has a rapidly expiring shelf life."[3]

Books investigating church decline and death seem to focus on how we might bring the younger generation back or persuade them to come for the first time. This analysis ignores what I believe is the fundamental problem: *Churches that cannot empathize with the faith journeys and wilderness times of baby boomers will not survive much longer*. If churches cannot offer a safe place to explore faith, then as voyages of exploration become more prevalent with later generations, the less connection the church makes with younger people. Although a person may be a fully devoted follower of Christ over their lifetime, how they express that trust in Christ changes through the different chapters of their life. They are engaging in "Good Faith Hunting."

Many churches have modeled themselves as a modernist, corporate organization. This organizational structure encourages the church leadership to approach congregants and attendees as if they were corporate employees. The attendees thus have a lower rank (or caste) than the church management and leadership. People's fears, questions, struggles, and changing views of faith do not help maintain the church leadership hierarchy as currently structured.

1. For examples see "Anne Rice Leaves Christianity," CNN Belief Blog; Bailey, "Q & A: Anne Rice on Following Christ Without Christianity."

2. Kunhardt, "Anne Rice: 'I Quit Being a Christian.'"

3. Barna, *Second Coming*, 1.

Good Faith Hunting is an age-old challenge and appears repeatedly in the biblical witness. Abram (Abraham), a seventy-five year old man, left his home to sojourn in an unknown land (Gen 12:1) long before he fully grasped all God told him. Moses hid for forty years (what a slacker!) as his father-in-law's shepherd (Exod 3). A rabble of slaves left Egypt terrified of their own shadows and through an epic adventure with God emerged as a cohesive people group, the Hebrews. Jonah ran from God's call and tried to vanish off the other end of the earth. Peter's understanding of following Christ unfolded as he confronted events, frequently stumbling and then being lifted up by Jesus Christ. Paul did not instantaneously become the Roman world's greatest evangelist after his life-altering Damascus road encounter. He spent time processing the event; studying, learning, and experimenting before he started writing his letters.

This is a book for church leaders and major influencers in a church who want to break out of the corporate, modernist mindset and celebrate faith growth through life, allegiance, and experience. It suggests ways to show the love of Christ as they sojourn alongside people in their community. Questions and doubts are part of the growth process and not a cause for fear. We as leaders and fellow pilgrims grow closer to people as we become a part of their lives and listen to their narratives of discovery. As leaders, we need to claim permission to admit we do not have all the answers nor can we cite biblical chapter and verse that explains it all. It is OK if we say, "I don't know why. I can't explain it."

David Kinnaman captures the concept and challenge well:

> It is difficult for many faith leaders to relate fully to the spiritual lives of people who struggle with their faith, particularly those who are younger. Clergy are typically older than those going through significant questions about their faith and are less likely to have personally experienced a period of major faith re-orientation themselves. What's more, not every person goes through a crisis of faith, so individuals who are going through spiritual transitions often go unnoticed. *Staying in tune with people's questions and doubts—at whatever age they occur—is an increasingly important part of being an influential faith leader.*[4]

In *A Churchless Faith*, one of the best studies on the subject, Alan Jamieson thoroughly examined the characteristics of highly committed

4. The Barna Group, "Do Americans Change Faith?" Italics added.

believers, mostly baby boomers, who abandoned church. Remarkably, he found that over ninety percent of the people who stopped attending church did not lose their core of Christian conviction, nor did they leave because of a reduced belief. Their faith was dynamic and transformed as life changes occurred.[5] Yet his research found that a large percentage of churches "through their structures, beliefs and faith packages, and particularly their public teaching, worship, and governance patterns encourage adults to become settled" and thus stagnant in their faith.[6] How many of these churches are fulfilling their Christ-given mission? How many are trying to preserve themselves as if they were a failing business by focusing inward and "circling the wagons"?

Ultimately, this book carries the message of faith and hope. Faith appears in surprising ways on the journey even when it appears to be absent. Maybe you know something needs to change but are not sure what to do next. Maybe you are reading this book because you are a leader and know that you seem to have stopped growing. Maybe you're in the wilderness, dry and lifeless, weary, burned out, not sure if your sermons matter at all, tired of putting up with the absurd demands of your denominational office, thinking about quitting, about to be fired, or living with the thousands of other reasons being a church leader isn't what you thought you signed up for. Yet, remarkably you still know that Jesus Christ is truly who he said he was. You're just not sure if the church you know recognizes Christ as the head.

Along the way in this book, you will discover ways of identifying the faith stages we progress through in life. We know the Bible is a rich source of journey narratives. Here you will find a sampling of prominent accounts as they relate to your own life story. Following Christ forces us into treks of exploration—we are *following* Christ, after all. "Anyone who intends to come with me has to let me lead. You're not in the driver's seat; *I* am" (Matt 16:24 MSG). Within these pages, we also fly over the wisdom of the desert fathers and mothers as they share their insights and guide us on our paths. The medieval mystics embraced faith excursions with some of the most profound insights ever written.

Interspersed between the chapters are stories of baby boomers and their trips through the faith landscape. Each of us has a distinctive

5. Jamieson, *A Churchless Faith*, 12. Jamieson's home country of New Zealand experienced a baby boom at roughly the same time as the United States.

6. Jamieson, *Ibid.*, 122.

narrative since we are all unique children of God. Some illustrate people that persevered through great despair and tribulation. Others are rich in wisdom within the framework of otherwise mundane events. We find common threads in the tapestries woven by other people's lives; we recognize the handiwork of God and the commonality of community that all of us possess.

You are not alone while embarking on your quest of discovery. Christ appears to us when we least expect it and he stays with us always even when we do not think he is there. We may not see the evidence until much later. I never did warm up to the music of the Grateful Dead, but the line, "What a long, strange trip it's been" from their song, "Truckin" has always stuck with me. We can explore the "long, strange trip" together, discovering Christ unexpectedly along the way.

1

How Did We Get Here?

All these thirsty people and no watering hole.

—Julia Duin, *Quitting Church*

What's Wrong with this Picture?

I recently spoke with Dave, a ministry leader who shared the following story.[1] He was checking references for Joe, a potential hire into Dave's parachurch organization. Joe received glowing references from numerous people who spoke about his leadership skills and how Joe reached into the community, helped ex-offenders reintegrate into the community by opening his house to them, led Bible studies for homeless people, and embodied a personal walk with Christ. However, when Dave, the interviewer, called Joe's pastor, he heard a markedly different account. The pastor said he was unsure of Joe's Christian walk because he saw Joe only during the weekly worship service and Joe rarely attended other church activities. Actually, Joe was busy in other areas of ministry beyond the church walls; the pastor failed to notice.

Joe is a baby boomer. Along with countless other members of his generation, each has had to ask himself or herself, *"Does my faith lie in the church as an institution, or does it lie in the person of Jesus Christ?"*

1. The names have been disguised in this story.

Quite possibly, the first generation born in modern times to do so, they are embracing the biblical idea of faith as a lifelong journey with inherent detours and wilderness times, *alongside* the organized church, rather than from *within* it. The dramatic sociological changes since the 1960s and the ongoing transition out of the enlightenment era force baby boomers to re-evaluate the meaning of faith.

George Barna reports that baby boomers "have been leaving the church in droves and expressing general dissatisfaction with conventional churches."[2] Over the last twenty years, church attendance among that generation has dropped by 12 percent while volunteering has declined by 10 percent.[3]

Seemingly, all of the doctrinal, political, social, or socioeconomic segments within Christianity have suffered major membership and attendance declines. The era of megachurches is passing as seen in mergers, staff layoffs, and church closings. Conservative evangelical groups are losing ground. Historically growing denominations such as the Southern Baptists report a decline in attendance.[4] Some thought the more socially liberal groups would maintain their attendance better than conservative groups. However, even the Episcopal Church, which made the largest liberal shift of the mainline denominations, reported a 23 percent decline in attendance over the last decade. That loss is similar to the declines reported in other mainline denominations. "Practically every denomination—Methodist, Lutheran, Presbyterian—that has tried to adapt itself to contemporary liberal values has seen an Episcopal-style plunge in church attendance."[5]

Between 2003 and 2007, Willow Creek Community Church, one of the premier baby boomer megachurches, undertook a series of surveys to answer the question, "Could scientific research help us understand and perhaps measure spiritual growth?"[6] The Willow Creek staff conducted extensive face-to-face interviews and then expanded the effort with almost 5,000 e-mail questionnaires. The survey showed that Willow Creek was not "creating fully devoted followers of Christ." The results surprised and unsettled Willow Creek leaders and churches

2 Barna, "Comments."

3. Barna, "Barna Describes Religious Changes."

4. Stetzer, "First-Person."

5. Douthat, "Can Liberal Christianity Be Saved?"

6. Hawking and Parkinson, *Reveal*, 91–93.

that followed their model because the results indicated no connection between increased and continued participation in church activities and spiritual growth. People more involved in church activities showed no greater love for God than those less involved. Increasing the number of programs and activities actually impeded people's growth in faith. Trends evident within Willow Creek are similar to comments from other baby boomer ministries.

Jack Miles, the author of *God: A Biography* had numerous conversations with people on his book promotion tours. He identified a common thread, especially with baby boomers,

> Over time, what struck me most about these conversations was a note of defiance, the defiant rejection of the widespread assumption that doubt and religion are incompatible. "Take it (belief) or leave it (religion)"—this was the dilemma I heard brusquely rejected in favor of a third alternative: *If I may doubt the practice of medicine from the operating table, if I may doubt the political system from the voting booth, if I may doubt the institution of marriage from the conjugal bed, why may I not doubt religion from the pew?*[7]

Recently an active layperson and baby boomer said after a very frustrating meeting, "We should be known as a church of *do's*, not a church of *don'ts*." If people in the congregation must ask permission before embarking on ministry, has their leadership decided the pastor is the head rather than Jesus Christ? For example, some churches use most of their resources focusing on worship services. Baby boomers and others question whether making sure drapes and furniture match the master worship plan even matters. They wonder if the church is mastering the details and missing the larger picture.

7. Miles, "Religion Makes a Comeback," 58. Italics added.

Generations, Generations

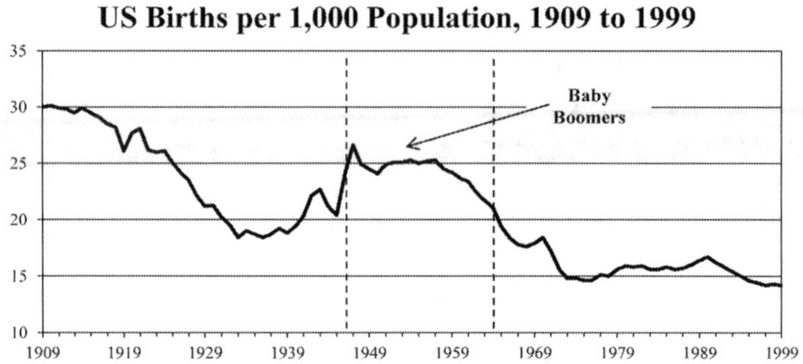

Figure 1. United States Birth Rates, 1909 to 1999[8]

The vastly increased birth rate during the baby boomer generation resulted in profound changes in the larger society. In the 1950s, local governments built schools at an unprecedented rate anticipating a major increase in school aged children. Buster Brown shoes, Gerber Baby Food, and the advice of Dr. Spock pointed the way to raise baby boomer children. Those of us in the early baby boomer or Vietnam cohort, born between 1946 and 1955, remember the headiness of the youth based counterculture of the 1960s. Beatlemania, new musical genres, civil rights movement, Vietnam War protests, Woodstock, and the "Summer of Love" epitomized the era. Many of us who were adolescents and young adults during the 1960s believed the song lyrics from the 1968 musical Hair: "This is the dawning of the Age of Aquarius." We embraced the mantra, "Don't trust anyone over thirty."

The promise of positive change quickly vanished. The "Summer of Love" quickly became the "Fall of Homelessness and Drug Abuse." The increasing conflicts over the Vietnam War polarized United States politics and society. The political assassinations, riots, protests, changing sexual mores, and drug experimentation combined into irresistible forces dramatically reshaping society in the United States and many other western nations. These major cultural trends started building earlier in the twentieth century. The Great Depression and World War II masked the effects and deferred their impacts several decades.

8. Centers for Disease Control and Prevention, *Live Births*, 1.

Wade Roof writes about the social and political turmoil of the 1960s:

> Few historians would question, in fact, that the ten-year period from President Kennedy's assassination in 1963 to Watergate in 1973 was one of the most turbulent, chaotic periods of American history, which left its imprint on the entire society, and particularly on those at a formative stages of their lives at the time. A major consequence was the plummeting of confidence among the young in all the dominant social institutions—political, economic, cultural, and religious. Politically, that loss of confidence is well known and associated with declines in voting and lack of party loyalty; religiously, it is less obvious but yet catastrophic in some ways.[9]

Those born between 1956 and 1964 form the second baby boomer cohort, sometimes called "Generation Jones." They inherited many of the detrimental results of the 1960s such as Watergate and President Nixon's resignation, the oil embargo and gasoline shortages, high inflation, and general economic malaise. The institutional mistrust emerging in the 1960s became more prominent during the 1970s.

The generational split between the builders and the baby boomers is deep. The builders learned about life during the Great Depression and World War II when many people had little control over the direction of their lives. They were constrained by global crises and circumstances. The low economic base and high unemployment during the Great Depression forced many people into unexpected deprivation that typically continued until World War II. When the builders looked at their children at protests and concerts sporting radically different dress and values, they could not understand why their children rejected the parents' music, values, and culture. The large gulf between baby boomers and their builder parents remains. Unfortunately, their parents designed the structure of traditional churches and especially those in mainline denominations.

The title of the 1965 Rolling Stones song, "I Can't Get No Satisfaction," captures many baby boomers' view about the church. Mick Jagger commented on the song: "It captures a spirit of the times, which is very important in those kinds of songs. . . . Which was alienation. Or it's a bit more than that, maybe, but a kind of sexual alienation. Alienation's

9. Roof, *Spiritual Marketplace*, 51.

not quite the right word, but it's one word that would do."[10] Paradoxically the idea of a "personal relationship with Christ" or the "sinner's prayer" being the *full encapsulation of Christianity* lead to even further alienation by de-emphasizing community life in Christ. If we follow these ideas to their logical conclusion, then each of us can be alone with Christ, totally separated from each other in our hermetic cocoon. How is this separation compatible with what Jesus said? "For where two or three come together in my name, there am I with them" (Matt 18:20).

As we transition out of the enlightenment, modernist, or Gutenberg age,[11] those generations that follow the baby boomers continue the transition to seeking truth in relationships and rejecting truth in propositions. Ironically, younger people deeply understand the implications of the "personal relationship with Christ" message, though many reject the message because it excludes community. The next conclusion they reach, whether warranted or not, is inescapable and devastating: *true community is rare in Christian congregations.*

Christian Belief and Growth

Business planners use the concept of *barriers to entry* when they analyze new growth opportunities. They ask if new product areas require large capital investments, specialized knowledge, access to specialized suppliers/distribution channels, governmental approval, or other factors that make entry more difficult. When we define Christian faith as a set of "propositional statements," we create the Christian version of barriers to entry. Whatever inhibits access to active participation or to a vibrant life in Christ's body inhibits becoming or growing as a follower of Christ. Too often, the process of "joining a church" becomes a barrier to entry that discourages a person from seeking a life journey with Christ. Before welcoming new members into a community, churches often require the newcomer to take a hard and fast position on the nature of divine inspiration, one's position on the end times, beliefs about

10. Songfacts, "(I Can't Get No) Satisfaction."

11. Sweet, *Viral*, 1-9. Len Sweet uses the term "Googlers" referring to younger generations who grew up in a relationship-based, connected world. "Gutenbergers" mean those baby boomer and prior generations who grew up in a print-based, propositional, and modernist world. The Googler phase is a way station as we transition into new ways of thinking.

the role of women in the church, and how much work the new member is doing toward trying to please God. Giving the right answers is essential; otherwise, those coming in might "contaminate" those within the church with wrong belief and clearly, we who are "inside" cannot fellowship with such misguided people. *How frequently do these barriers to entry exclude people who sincerely desire to follow Christ?*

Len Sweet and Frank Viola's solution is elegant and basic. They define "Christian" very simply, cutting through the excess baggage. "So what is Christianity? It is Christ. Nothing more. Nothing less. Christianity is the 'good news' that beauty, truth, and goodness are found in a person [Jesus Christ]."[12] Christianity is never a proposition. In *I Am a Follower*, Len restates the definition in a slightly different form, "There may be more to being a Christian than followership. There certainly cannot be less."[13]

Changes occur in life. People realize that decisions have consequences, parents age and die, workers lose jobs, children leave home, and good health declines with age. Baby boomers face their own finitude. Faith develops or evolves through life stages and a person's perception of God and Christ changes over their life. These life stages affect our relationships to a church and with others. Denial of change ignores the biblical witness about transformation. The Hebrews' wilderness wanderings were a key factor in precipitating their transformation from a group of slaves to a cohesive people group.

The biblical witness suggests that faith is a journey, a series of stages moving along a variety of trajectories rather than a static pathway. The concept of a faith expedition is inherently relational because the path cannot be precisely defined or categorized. The journey may have solitary times but other phases may occur together in community. A brief overview of the changes in the ways of thinking may bring greater understanding of why Christian faith manifests itself in journey for baby boomers and other generations.

12. Sweet and Viola, *Jesus Manifesto*, xvi.

13. Sweet, *I Am a Follower*, 20.

Modernity and Postmodernity

We are currently in a major epistemological (*way of thinking*) shift as profound as the transition from medieval to enlightenment, or modernist thought. Modernist thought emphasizes the autonomy of the individual and elevates science as an abstract discipline. Its fruits include an increasing standard of living stemming from increased wealth, a reduction in monarchies into more egalitarian governments, and remarkable technological advances.

The precursor to enlightenment thinking that allowed the wide dissemination of ideas was the invention of movable type printing and the printing press by Johannes Gutenberg in about 1439. This invention allowed the rapid dissemination of ideas from distant regions and changed the entire systems of social, governmental, ecclesiastical, and scientific interactions. Without the printing press, a Bible would have remained a rare and precious treasure, controlled by a priestly hierarchy. Radical ideas, such as new ways of thinking about the universe and God, would have remained within small groups of scholars. Three hundred thousand copies of Martin Luther's *Ninety-Five Theses* entered circulation within two years of its 1517 writing. The wide distribution was the instigating event for the Protestant reformation. *Ninety-Five Theses* also inadvertently triggered the proliferation of denominations and separations based on minor doctrinal differences that continues unabated today.

In the following centuries of philosophical transition, enlightenment thinking had its origins in the work of René Descartes in the fourteenth century and later extended by Immanuel Kant in the eighteenth century. Descartes started from a position of doubt and sought certainty at deeper and deeper levels. His breakthrough came when he formulated the famous phrase, "*Cogito ergo sum*," or "I think, therefore I am."[14] He added a secondary argument that humans could not exist possessing the idea of God unless they derived their existence from God. Descartes' formulation interpreted Genesis 1:27, "So God created man in his own image," to mean that God gave people intellect in the image of God. The era of modernity emphasized reason and individualism rather than tradition, which was more a mark of the preceding medieval age.

14. "Descartes," *Concise OED*.

The limits to enlightenment thinking began to appear in the last century and philosophers struggled to define a new framework, currently called postmodern or emergent thinking. Jean-François Lyotard defined postmodern or emergent thinking as "incredulity towards metanarratives."[15] *Metanarrative* means the overarching framework that makes sense of such fields as history and progress. In postmodern thinking, interpretation of narrative and story becomes localized and specific to a community. The philosophy rejects or offers a corrective to the perceived excesses of modernity. Modernity advocates claim to operate in a sphere of "scientific detachment" as rational observers, but actually assume an understanding of knowing that defines the desired objectives and the results achieved.

One of the premier observers of this shift in philosophy, Michael Polanyi argues for "*personal participation* of the knower in all acts of understanding."[16] Walter Brueggemann states, "Christian interpretation in preaching and liturgy is *contextual, local, and pluralistic*."[17] This definition implies a different lens for reading Genesis 1:27: "So God created man in his own image, in the image of God he created them, male and female he created them." Descartes would focus on the singular resulting in *cogito ergo sum* while Brueggemann would focus on the plural, "He created *them*." In postmodernism and the related philosophical shifts, relationship is the core of creation in the image of God while in modernity knowledge or the intellect is the core.

The social transitions of the baby boomer generation reflect this shift in thinking and the increasing rejection of modernist thought. No longer is the church in an environment with one interpretation of scripture. A set of propositions cannot define God or Christ, thus scripture returns to its original polyvalent roots. The interpretation develops dependent upon the community.

Churches struggle with this transition and thus struggle in dealing with people who have different understandings of scripture and doctrines. Much of the western Christian church is strongly "Gutenberg print based" while the culture of younger generations is "story, image, and sound based." Baby boomers are the main transition generation and struggle to conform into a print world transitioning to a symbolic

15. Lyotard, *The Postmodern Condition*, xxiv.

16. Polanyi, *Personal Knowledge*, vii.

17. Brueggemann, *Texts*, 9.

world. Increasingly, the print output of churches connects less and less with baby boomers on their faith journey because the print poorly expresses the concepts of faith explorations and sojourns.

A Proposed Solution

When we focus on atonement and the "sinner's prayer" as the single meaningful event and single proposition in Christian faith, we fall into the trap Karl Marx warned about: religion can be the "opiate of the masses."[18] Marx believed religion that emphasized the afterlife to the exclusion of justice and mercy in this current life enabled the Russian aristocrats' oppression and mistreatment of peasants.

Some modernist versions of evangelical Christianity promote "fire insurance" for eternal salvation while ignoring the kingdom of God (Mark 1:15, Luke 17:21) available in life. Those versions have an incomplete view of the Christian faith. Those belief systems stress the priestly aspect of Christ's message emphasizing his sacrifice for atonement and salvation to the diminution of the rest of the Gospel. The Gospel, or Good News, extends throughout the entire Bible and is not limited to Matthew, Mark, Luke, and John. The Good News includes creation and re-creation into the image of God. We receive a call to act justly and with mercy. We leave slavery into liberation, and when we go into exile, Christ restores us after our wanderings. We participate with God by moving from bondage into freedom. We move from freedom into exile and then back into freedom again.

The desire to "check the box" by having someone say the "sinner's prayer" to the exclusion of becoming a disciple and follower reflects an obsession with atonement. Recitation of the prayer confirms some evangelicals' sense of task-based success and does not require involvement in converts' lives. If converts seek growth and maturity, do churches become uncomfortable with their questions and their desire to show faith in action? In my experience, too many churches discourage such explorations, possibly from fear that the questions asked will lead the convert further away from Christ. However, Christ encouraged penetrating and risky questions. He asked his disciples a direct question

18. Stackhouse and Miller, "Economic Ethics," 2:17–18.

that drilled deep into the nature of Jesus himself: "But who do you say that I am?" (Matt 16:15).

In Mark, one of the teachers of the law asked Jesus which commandment was most important. "The most important one,' answered Jesus, 'is this: 'Hear, O Israel, the Lord our God, the Lord is one. Love the Lord your God with all your heart and with all your soul and with all your mind and with all your strength.' The second is this: 'Love your neighbor as yourself.' There is no commandment greater than these" (Mark 12:29–31). Relationships with people have the same importance as a relationship with God. One without the other is incomplete and leads to a human interpreted Gospel (or good news) missing key elements.

An Analytical Framework

Stages of Faith by James Fowler proposed six Stages of Faith, closely related to psychological development theories as a framework for examining how a person's faith transitions through life. Fowler defines faith, rather than belief or religion, as the fundamental element in connecting us to transcendent realities. Belief and religion are secondary, following faith. We owe a large debt to Alan Jamieson, who built upon Fowler's framework in researching people that left evangelical and Pentecostal churches.[19] Many leaders assume those who leave a church lack mature faith and fall away from Christianity; however, Jamieson's initial interviews with church leavers surprised him. He met people who had been highly involved in the church's ministry but who developed a general malaise and dissatisfaction. Jamieson reports that those people rarely turned away from Christian faith; instead, they embarked on a journey to discover their faith. Many people wandered in a wilderness state for months or years, but usually Christian faith remained a very important part of their lives. They may disagree with their particular denominations or theological roots, but 90 percent report their faith as unambiguously Christian.

Jamieson uses a metaphor of a swim club that meets at the beach to help explain those who go exploring the depths of their faith. The swimmers playing in the water look very exciting to someone going

19. Jamieson, *Chrysalis*, 23–24. Evangelical Pentecostal charismatic is Jamieson's term describing the churches he researched.

to the beach for the first time. A newcomer joins the swim club, learns what it offers. He or she experiences great joy in the activities. Eventually, the newcomer looks at the buoys marking the edge of the club and wonders what is beyond. The individual may meet a group of deep-sea anglers who tell amazing tales of life in the deep. The individual longs to explore the unsafe waters beyond the boundaries and becomes discontent and disillusioned. People in the swim club sense this attraction, and suggest the individual attend more swim meets. The swim meets relieve the discontent temporarily, but the unsettled sense returns even more pronounced.

Then the individual pushes beyond the boundaries and begins exploration of wild and unknown areas. The individual senses danger everywhere, but continues the exciting exploration. The explorer investigates every new beach, island, waterfall, cove, and current. The journey continues without a specific destination, and the exploration brings great pleasure. The dangers and wonder of surprising unknowns magnify the swimmer's appreciation of swimming. Whirlpools and rip currents could drown the devotee, but survival in the company of a small group of fellow swimmers gives strength and makes the dangers worthwhile.

Jamieson's research demonstrates that the majority of people who journey from the church remain in the Christian faith, which implies the need for only a rough map with outlines of waypoints and semi-defined outcomes. A well-defined and scripted journey may have less value. For example, a tour group with a closely defined schedule typically offers a tame voyage with restricted adventure and discovery. Journeyers see new things, but well-defined outcomes may limit their awe and wonder. Other non-scripted types of journeys allow detours, visits to people's homes, walks beyond tourist areas, explorations, and schedule changes. These baby boomers and people of other generations sense adventure, look into rarely seen places, experience the world with all their sensations, and learn new appreciations of how God works.

—For Reflection—

1. Where do you fit in the generations?
2. How well do you understand people of older generations? What about younger generations?
3. Re-read the quotation from Jack Miles on page 3. Do you agree with it? Why or why not?
4. Imagine a time of journey in your life. Was it scary? Was it exhilarating? Did you feel lost and alone? What did God show you through that time?

2

Stages of Faith and Church Leavers

Faith is not always religious in its content or context. To ask these questions seriously of oneself or others does not necessarily mean to elicit answers about religious commitment or belief. Faith is a person's or group's way of moving into the force field of life.

—James Fowler, *Stages of Faith*

Stages of Faith

When we consider how faith or belief changes over a lifetime, we need a framework to analyze people's movement. James Fowler's *Stages of Faith* and Alan Jamieson's study of church leavers give us signposts and celestial markers so we can navigate the pathways and changes we observe over a person's lifetime. Stages of Faith are like rings of a tree that build on each other. A young child has a very concrete and literal faith. A teenager builds faith by looking further afield yet remains concrete. Adults transition through the tree rings, morphing as they undergo trials and maturing in their faith walk.

What is faith? How is it different from belief? Is belief or faith more foundational to the journey of following Christ? The writer of Hebrews says, "Now faith is being sure of what we hope for and certain of what we do not see" (Heb 11:1). Expressing faith as a noun is a poor representation of the underlying premises. In fact, the Old Testament has no noun for faith. It is best defined as a verb, a Hebraic sense of "to be" in meaning. Eugene Peterson writes, "When God spoke to Moses at the burning bush in Midian and Moses asked him for his name, the answer he got was not a name."[1] God responded to Moses saying "*ehyeh asher ehyeh*" *or* "I AM WHO I AM" (Exod 3:14). "I am" is the first person form of *hayah*, "to be." "I AM" is the whole of creation and humanity is part of it.

Faith is about one's state of being in relationship with Christ, with others, and with himself or herself in the context of daily living. Faith is an inherently relational action verb. It does not happen solely as a "me and Jesus" experience nor is the statement "my faith is private to me" meaningful. Faith is an intersecting set of three circles that includes the individual, the transcendent truth that *is* Christ, and other people.

Belief, on the other hand, turns faith into an abstract concept that allows us to compartmentalize life. We can "believe in" something and never confront the implications of that belief. If we have belief, we can show up for worship services and talk about how much it spoke to our heart while completely forgetting the point of the message the next day. Belief compartmentalizes life into spirit and reality. Belief falls into the category of spirit. Driving to work and mundane life falls into the category of reality. Westerners tend to split the two without ever thinking about disconnects between them.

We can try harder to believe, knowing that if we just study the Bible intently, we will achieve full belief. What will happen when we achieve full belief? Maybe we will enter the Christian equivalent of *nirvana*, fully blown out like a candle, entering total emptiness, and leaving behind all that makes us human. Few Christ followers have taken the time to differentiate between faith and belief. We hear a lot about growing in the faith, but who really knows what that means? Leaving behind "beliefs" for a moment, we will focus instead on what it means to journey into a stronger and deeper faith, "being in relationship" with Christ.

Growth, transitions, and morphing faith are normal parts of life. In the Christian church, we usually segregate children by age, much as our schools do, because their maturity and understanding changes as they grow up. Congregations spend millions of dollars on curriculum each year to make sure the message connects with the children.

1. Peterson, *Practice Resurrection*, Kindle e-book, location 2780.

If we differentiate based on maturity and understanding for children, should we not do the same for adults who are continuing to grow? Churches sometimes attempt to segment adults based on marital status or age, but rarely attempt to tailor curriculum based on their faith growth. The apostle Paul gives us a challenge. "When I was a child, I talked like a child, I thought like a child, I reasoned like a child. When I became a man, I put childish ways behind me. Now we see but a poor reflection as in a mirror; then we shall see face to face. Now I know in part; then I shall know fully" (1 Cor 13:11–12). *How do we invite the Holy Spirit in to help us connect with people on different sections of a faith trek?*

Fowler's Six Stages of Faith

Stages of Faith by James Fowler recognized the differences between belief and faith, providing a framework for examining how a person's faith undergoes transitions through life. "Faith, rather than belief or religion, is the most fundamental category in the human quest for relation to transcendence. Faith, it appears, is generic, a universal feature of human living, recognizably similar everywhere despite the remarkable variety of forms and contents of religious practice and belief."[2] He concludes that the faith development process is independent of a person's belief system because belief and religion are secondary, driven by faith. There is nothing inherently Christian or even monotheistic about the faith development process. The same process applies if a person "believes" in science, the environment, social systems, the nation, materialism, or other overarching transcendent realities.

The separation of faith and belief is a key element in Fowler's work because the framework applies independently of belief systems and doctrinal differences. *Faith is not a simple assent to a propositional belief or truth but rather the entire collection of a person's intellect, feelings, and way of being.* He presents the basis for the faith stages: "These stages, which try to describe uniform and predictable *ways* of being in faith, are not primarily matters of the *contents* of faith."[3]

2. Fowler, *Stages of Faith*, 14.

3. Fowler, *Becoming Adult*, 52.

Fowler's research pointed to a set of six faith stages. The stages always occur in order so higher numbered stages always follow lower numbered stages. Each stage builds on the previous stages and no stage skipping occurs. Adults typically stop their transitions between Stage 3 and Stage 5. Stage 6 is very rare.

Stage 1, called *Intuitive-Projective Faith*, "is the fantasy-filled, imitative phase in which the child can be powerfully and permanently influenced by examples, moods, actions, and stories of the visible faith of primally related adults."[4] The term *primally related* refers to adults who are in a very close relationship with the child. It begins at approximately age two or three. At this age children have independent mobility, begin to develop language ability, and can investigate and question by themselves. Self is the center of experience, with no internally developed models for understanding experiences. The transition to the next stage involves differentiation between real events and fantasy life.

Stage 2, called *Mythic-Literal Faith*, exhibits a strong confidence in the fairness, justice, and reciprocity of the universe. Beliefs, moral rules, and attitudes have literal interpretations. The ultimate environment of the universe has a "built-in, divinely constituted, natural lawfulness."[5] Stage 2 includes the ability to understand the perspective of others, which leads to a strong sense of fairness. The size of the child's world widens to include school, peers, television, movies, internet, reading, and related arenas. Because of this expansion, the variety of influences that affect the child increase. Children typically make strong associations with "people like us" as opposed to those who are different.

The first two stages are typically part of the childhood and early teenage years; however, some adults remain in Stage 2. They continue to view the world literally and have difficulty accepting differences in their world. A delayed move from Stage 2 to Stage 3 generates a perceived lack of fairness when the person moves into adulthood. I have encountered this faith stage frequently in prison chaplaincy. Many higher security inmates assume that everybody is out to "get" them. The initial response is to "get" others before they are "gotten" themselves. The aggressor has much higher status in prison culture than the target of the aggression.

4. Fowler, *Stages of Faith*, 133.

5. Ibid., 149–150.

Stage 3, *Synthetic-Conventional Faith*, the first truly adult faith stage, is a time when "a number of spheres demand attention: family, school or work, peers, street society and media, and perhaps religion. . . . Faith must synthesize values and information; it must provide a basis for identity and outlook."[6] This stage arises in adolescence and is frequently a permanent place in adulthood. Fowler uses "synthetic" to mean that the individual attempts to draw together the various parts of life into an integrated identity. The individual now operate in a number of spheres such as work, school, and family. Faith is conventional because the person derives values and beliefs from peer groups or significant others. A Stage 3 person typically accepts those beliefs strongly with little examination: "[Individuals at this stage are] acutely tuned to the expectations and judgments of significant others, and as yet do not have a sure enough grasp of their own identity and autonomous judgment to construct and maintain an independent perspective. . . . At Stage 3 a person has an 'ideology,' a more or less consistent clustering of values and beliefs, but he or she has not objectified it for examination and in a sense is unaware of having it."[7]

Fowler believes symbol and ritual are the main ways of interacting and finding meaning with the transcendent in Stage 3. Religious organizations such as churches function well in their institutional role if a high percentage of their adherents are in Stage 3. Leaders are the sources of meaning as trusted external authority figures, and adherents have a strong sense of loyalty and are committed workers. Innovative thinking and questioning is rare at this stage.

Stage 4, *Individuative-Reflective Faith*, is a time of tensions and struggle. The person develops individual identity and worldview, differentiated from others, and internally recognized. The transition between Stage 3 and 4 typically occurs in the early to mid-20s; however, for some people it comes in their 30s and 40s, if at all.[8] The transition involves two essential factors. First, there must be a shift away from the previous value system: "The 'tyranny of the they'—or the potential for it—must

6. Ibid., 172.

7. Ibid., 173.

8 Fowler's research occurred in the 1970s so these ages are meaningful for baby boomers. However, the accelerating pace of change in later generations suggests that at least from a transcendent religious standpoint, these transitions may be occurring at earlier ages.

be undermined."[9] Individuals must be willing to break away from the crowd, or question the positions of previously revered authority figures. The person takes responsibility for actions rather than accepting externally imposed values. Personal decision-making becomes important for people in Stage 4.

Stage 4 individuals respond to different leadership methods from those in Stage 3. Independence is valued over dependency, and they struggle with a leadership style that encourages dependence. Criticism and debate is more accepted, and they entertain the serious questions of underlying meaning.

Stage 5, *Conjunctive Faith*, typically not reached before mid-life, acknowledges paradox and transcendence, reuniting reality and symbolic/conceptual meanings in a "second naïveté." Stage 5 requires that persons know the sacrament of defeat and the consequences of irrevocable commitments and acts. By this time friends or family members have died, which forces persons to consider the limited nature of life and the reality of death. Physical attributes and abilities change with the process of growing and looking older. Children reach teenage or adult years and frequently move away from home.

Fowler offers metaphors for Stage 5:

- Realizing that the behavior of light requires that it be understood both as a wave phenomenon *and* as particles of energy. . . . Discovering that the rational solution or "explanation" of a problem that seems so elegant is a painted canvas covering an intricate, endlessly intriguing cavern of surprising depth. . . . Looking at a field of flowers simultaneously through a microscope and a wide-angle lens.[10]
- A genuine openness [develops] to the truths of traditions and communities other than one's own. This openness, however, is not to be equated with a relativistic agnosticism (literally a not knowing). . . . This is to help overcome blind spots as well as the tendencies to idolatry (the over identification of our symbolizations of transcending truth with the reality of truth) to which all our traditions are prone.

9. Ibid., 179.
10. Ibid., 184.

- [There is] an awareness of the need to face and hold together several unmistakable *polar tensions* in one's life: the polarities of being both *old* and *young* and of being both *masculine* and *feminine*. Further it means integrating the polarity of being both *constructive* and *destructive* and the polarity of having a conscious and a shadow self.
- Conjunctive faith gives rise to a second naiveté, a post critical receptivity and readiness for participation in the reality brought to expression in symbol and myth.[11]

Stage 6, *Universalizing Faith*, is extremely rare. One's ultimate environment is inclusive of all being. Fowler describes two key items in the transition to universalizing faith: a de-centering combined with a widening of the circle of important voices. These individuals view the world through the eyes of those who are quite different from themselves. Persons in Stage 6 move the locus of value away from their personal values. Their sense of the common good outweighs personal good, even at the expense of their own safety. Only rare people with the characteristics of a Mother Teresa, Dietrich Bonhoeffer, Martin Luther King, and Mahatma Gandhi achieve this transition. These individuals give up self for the sake of the community.

Criticisms of Stages of Faith

One of the concerns in classic evangelical arenas is that approaching faith as a journey minimizes the salvific nature of believers' relationship with Christ. The church leadership of such congregations asks itself, "If faith continues to 'grow,' will it 'outgrow' dependence on Christ?" This fear arises because major parts of the evangelical church find themselves in a dead-end corner. That dead-end is the assumption of salvation in Christ as the final or only important event in a person's walk with Christ during this life rather than the first event and part of a process. If salvation is the only important event, it precludes the need for personal growth and renders growth undesirable from a church's standpoint.

The concept of a theological journey may frighten those who hold this view because it implies persons' change throughout their lives, and they might leave their current church as they grow and change. Church

11. Ibid., 64–65.

leaders fear loss of church membership if people grow in their walk with God, which may signal good reasons for leaving that church. This fear infects leaders in churches that do not turn loose disciples to go out into the world. These leaders keep congregants dependent because loss of members and control implies personal loss of prestige.

A number of postmodern thinkers hold that form and content are inseparable in the areas of self-definition, faith, and belief. Faith is not meaningful separate from experience in an individual's life and thus structural analysis of faith is misapplied. Paradoxically, the recognition of different faith stages is postmodern. Faith and faith journeys are inherently relational rather than propositional.

Movement between stages is painful and lonely, and the dismantling and reconstruction of an earlier belief superstructure is uncomfortable. If all the individual receives from their church is more exhortation to re-apply the "sinner's prayer," then the stage transitions become exceedingly difficult. Beliefs may not change, but people's understandings of those beliefs can change. Individuals' movement from a mono-cultural tribal church environment to a more independent existence may remove them from the comfort of shared values, cultures, and experiences. They may believe they are losing their Christian faith because the worship service no longer seems relevant. For example, previously enlightening pastoral messages become dull and boring, the music seems stale and repetitive, and church activities bring no joy.

Fowler does not address the transitions between the stages. His research deals with people who are in stable or semi-stable stages and focuses on persons between Stages 2 and 5. The transition between the Stage 4 individualism and Stage 5 re-focusing on community is particularly difficult and is a major turning point for some baby boomers in their faith journey as they age. As we will see in the next section, many people leave the church during the Stage 4 to Stage 5 transition.

Church Leavers

Like James Fowler, Alan Jamieson's research verified that faith is not a static concept. It is dynamic and changes as a person experiences life in its triumphs and disappointments, promises and unmet expectations, structure and surprises. In *A Churchless Faith*, Jamieson examined the characteristics of highly committed people who left evangelical,

Pentecostal, and charismatic churches in his home country of New Zealand. Remarkably, he found that over 90 percent of the people who stopped attending church did not lose their core of Christian faith, nor did they leave because of a reduced faith.

Jamieson interviewed church leavers during 1995 to 1996. The interviewees were mostly baby boomers who had not reached midlife, an age of major life stage transitions. Ninety-three percent of the people interviewed were between thirty and fifty years of age at the time, which aligns closely with the 1946 to 1964 baby boomer birth dates. [12]

Fowler's Stages of Faith provide a lens for understanding how respondents' faith changed during the leaving process and insight on whether they left the Christian faith. The figure below illustrates Jamieson's research compared with the Fowler faith stage of analysis.

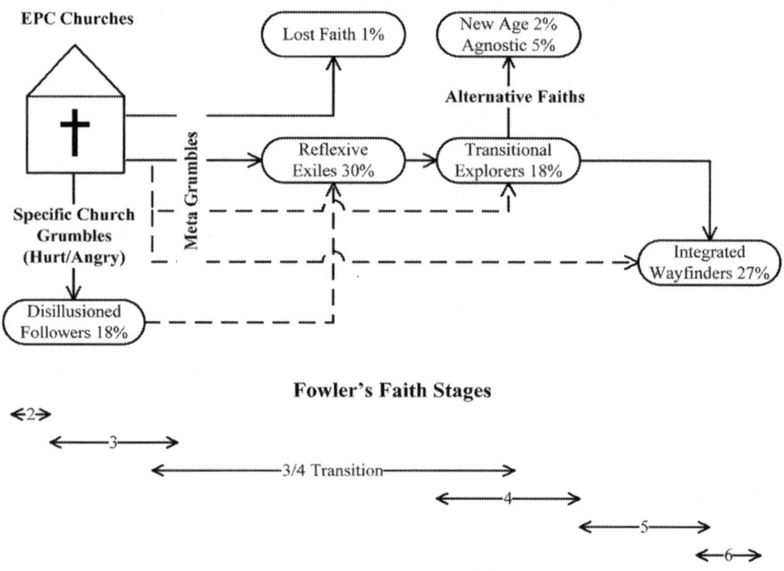

Figure 2. Jamieson's and Fowler's Categories Compared.[13]

Disillusioned Followers constituted about 18 percent the interviewees. They had left the church recently and remained hurt or angry about their church experience but did not question church doctrine or the basic faith tenets. "Reflexive Exiles" left church for different reasons and comprised 30 percent of respondents. They typically left over a

12. Jamieson, *A Churchless Faith*, 12.

13. Ibid., 123.

period of eighteen months or more and professed an increasing sense of unease and irrelevancy between the church, their foundational faith, and their lives. They have deep-seated uneasiness and questions about their foundational faith. "Transitional Explorers," 18 percent of leavers, are in the process of reconstructing a faith. They have retained portions of their previous faith, and have discarded aspects of their previous faith, replacing it with new insights. The members of this group are positive about their faith and show confidence in it. "Integrated Way-finders" have completed the task of reconstructing their faith into an integrated whole and include 23 percent of respondents. People in this group integrate their faith into all facets of their lives, and they are aware of their personal flaws that interfere with their faith. They have a more stable faith location that includes times of significant re-examination. These people are in a "second naïveté" in which they can accept paradox by understanding the deep-seated origins of those paradoxes.[14]

People in these groupings retained a core of Christian faith, regardless of how their journey unfolded. A small remainder of approximately 8 percent have moved out of a Christian core, with 1 percent defining themselves as atheist, 2 percent other religions, and 5 percent agnostic.

Faith Stages of Church Leavers

Jamieson's church leaver definitions correlate with Fowler's Stages of Faith. He places the churches he studied within Fowler's Stage 3, because those churches "through their structures, beliefs and faith packages, and particularly their public teaching, worship, and governance patterns encourage adults to become settled at this third stage."[15] A number of the individuals within these churches can be in Stage 4 or 5, but the public practices of the church direct them toward a Stage 3 group. Reflexive Exiles are associated with Stage 3 to Stage 4 transitions, while Transitional Explorers and Integrated Way-finders map to Stage 4 and Stages 5/6 respectively.

Jamieson discovered that the typical cause of leaving is not lack of Christian faith, but rather by disconnection between the objectives of the church organization and a deep, heart-felt call of God. Few of

14. Brueggemann, *Psalms*, 25.

15. Jamieson, *A Churchless Faith*, 122.

his study subjects rejected their Christian faith, although their views matured and no longer aligned with their former churches. Several observers joked that people leave the church to keep their faith.[16]

The earlier discussion of Fowler's Stages of Faith illustrates how these transitions are trigger points for faith re-evaluation, which suggests an accelerated pace of church leaving by aging baby boomers. Jamieson's study also suggests that active church attendees do not want to hear church leaders tell them to be quiet when they question policies and doctrine. For example, a few years ago I attended a regional meeting of a mainline Protestant denomination as a local church representative. During the discussion time, another participant and I spoke respectfully in opposition to the leadership's views on an issue under discussion. From the podium, the presiding officer told us to—using a few more words—"sit down and shut up." Initially, the vote on the issue was oral. However, the results were close enough that the leadership conducted a written ballot. The regional meeting upheld the presiding officer's position by a slight margin.

Jamieson's research also suggests that faith journeys will become more prevalent as baby boomers encounter clashes between life changes and the Stage 3 attractional model prevalent in many churches. Many of the baby boomer church leaders found faith in the 1960s and 1970s, a time in which Chuck Smith was founding Calvary Chapel, John Wimber was starting the Vineyard Movement, and the Jesus movement was at its peak. My sense is that those leaders subconsciously yearn for a repetition of the time when they came to faith. How many churches still maintain ghosts of the leaders' youth and inadvertently discourage people from growing? Will people grow within a church body or will they seek another community, allowing them to soar free as their wings strengthen?

—For Reflection—

1. When did you experience faith transitions in your life? What factors led to those transitions?
2. Are you in a transition now?
3. Where would you place yourself in Fowler's Stages? In Jamieson's definitions?

16. For other examples, see the interviews in Duin, *Quitting Church*.

3

My Journey

But Jonah got up and went the other direction to Tarshish, running away from God. He went down to the port of Joppa and found a ship headed for Tarshish. He paid the fare and went on board, joining those going to Tarshish—as far away from God as he could get.

—JONAH 1:3 *THE MESSAGE*

I WAS BORN IN Hampton, Virginia, in 1952, the oldest child with three younger sisters. My father was in the Air Force at the time. I remember sitting on the couch at the apartment when my father walked in from work one day and gave me a toy, but I do not know why he did. I don't remember anything special about the occasion nor do I remember him giving me gifts at other times. I'm not completely sure that is one of my memories or one I reconstituted from later conversations. Even at that age, he was distant to me and I don't remember conversations with him.

My father probably did not know how to relate with me. When he was young, his parents underwent a very public, high-society divorce during the depths of the Great Depression. One parent lost everything and became destitute, while the other parent remained well off. My father's mode and standard of living changed drastically based on which parent he lived with at any given time.

His childhood became a nightmare since he became a possession and weapon fought over by the two parents. He never knew from day-to-day where he would be living. On several occasions while walking home from school, private detectives kidnapped him off the street and took him to the other parent. One time I found newspaper clippings that my father saved describing the divorce. The custody battles over him received top billing in the article. I still regret that during his lifetime I never dug deeper with him into the pain he felt from his shattered childhood.

After my father finished his military service, we moved to Hendersonville, North Carolina, and lived in the same house as my mother's parents. Their house, built in the early part of the twentieth century, was located on two acres of land. The house had a basement mostly devoted to a coal hopper and furnace, a main floor with massive rooms, and a second floor with equally large bedrooms. Behind the house sat a stand-alone garage, a guest cottage, and an acre-sized garden started even further back. When we lived there, my grandfather gave me the best toy I ever received—an old plumbing faucet fixture. I would get wrenches from above the workbench, and then disassemble and reassemble my treasure for hours at a time.

Then we moved to Green Cove Springs, Florida so that both my parents could take positions as teachers. We attended the local Methodist church while we lived in Florida. Their service always started with the hymn, "Holy, Holy, Holy." Most of our music came from a scratchy and raspy record player. There may have been a piano or organ in the sanctuary, but I did not pay much attention to such items. A rack on the wall contained the hymn numbers for the day. The building had a typical Florida musty smell, a low ceiling, and a sloping floor so those in the back pews could easily see what was happening in the front.

I attended Sunday school, but I do not remember anything about it. My father was Sunday school superintendent. During this time, he constantly doubted the reality of God. He came to a profound and deep Christian conviction much later in life.

Later we moved back to Hendersonville when I entered the fifth grade. We attended the largest Methodist church in the area, a city congregation surrounded by numerous small rural congregations. I would describe the church as being theologically liberal, combined with being socially conservative. Anything that evoked the early history of the Methodists, such as "shouting Methodists," Holiness strains, or Pentecostal tendencies, struck great fear into the pastors. We dared not show too much "enthusiasm." I don't remember much in the way of revival preaching, or singing about being "washed the blood of the Lamb," talking much about judgment, salvation, or even considering the implications of a biblical passage. The church was a social gathering spot and the Sunday morning sermons put me to sleep. Staying awake was an exercise in torture! I am sure I had a cynical teenager attitude, but after compensating for that, I know the sermons were mostly "do-good" type messages devoid of deep meaning.

I undoubtedly remembered some of what I had heard in the youth group and Sunday School. One night I had a vivid dream, and I knew it was a visit from the Holy Spirit. I was crying like a baby in the middle of the dream. I did not hear any words but knew it was the Holy Spirit. I was afraid to share this experience with anyone at the church, lest I find myself in the category of "snake handlers" as we considered my Pentecostal friends at school. They had too much "enthusiasm" and believed weird things. At least I thought they were weird. Of course, I thought the Nazarenes were bizarre and outlandish too! I guess we were uptown Methodists, too "cultured" for other people.

Once I graduated from high school and left for college, I totally ignored Christianity. I cannot place my finger on the exact reason, but I seem to have gone through the same types of change and rejection of parents' value systems that was especially prevalent in the early 1970s. My first year of college was a disaster; I rarely attended classes and flunked out. I was in a degree program I hated. Finally, I realized I was an engineer at heart and graduated seven years later from Georgia Tech.

After graduation, I met and married my wife in 1978. Her father was one of the formative mentors in my life. He was both a work colleague and a guide who showed me how to accept adulthood responsibilities. He filled a missing piece in my life since my relationship with my own father was strained and difficult. My wife and I had three children by 1987, and we moved to California to follow my dream of importance in the engineering and management world.

We spent eight years in California—my wife jokes that we spent "four years living there and four years trying to get out." The first company I worked for in California declared bankruptcy. Thankfully, I did not have to look very hard for another job. We attended a church in California for three years, and left in frustration. The trauma kept us from attending any other church. When I found a job near Mesa, Arizona, we were thankful to leave California behind permanently.

In this new job, I started encountering work difficulties about a year later. I did not listen to others and connect with people. I could not resolve the resulting difficulties and the company fired me. My worth as a person stemmed from my excellence in the work force. My inability to solve the underlying difficulties destroyed my sense of self-worth. I was an engineer, after all, and paid to solve problems. Or so I thought that's how life should work. Maybe I was afraid that I would follow my father's example—very capable but never able to achieve success because of his expectation of failure stemming from childhood.

God used the firing to break what I perceived as a self-created disaster cycle, getting my attention, and readjusting my priorities. Like Jonah and the fish, my job loss focused my attention on God. In desperation, I finally cried out to Christ and said, "OK, whatever you want me to do now. I can't do it anymore on my own. I surrender."

Through this pain and time in the wilderness feeling totally out of control, God rebuilt my life with a different set of priorities. I am on an adventure that continues today with a radically different direction than the life voyage I had planned. Out of this pain and loss, God provided many part-time ministry opportunities along with a full-time job that is much better suited to my talents.

At roughly the same time, I met an unusual fellow over the Christmas season. I wrote an article about the experience for *The United Methodist Reporter*.

The Messenger

> "Do not forget to entertain strangers, for by so doing some people have entertained angels without knowing it" (Heb. 13:2).
>
> On a Saturday during the Christmas season, a call came into the church from a young man who needed to talk to someone.
>
> All of our pastors were either on vacation or unavailable, so after several referrals, I ended up talking to him on the phone and agreed to meet him in a sports bar across town.
>
> He was a musician from Colorado and was heading for a city 50 miles away from Mesa to do advance work for a praise band. He was wearing a dirty T-shirt and needed a bath. He was totally out of money, and the band's equipment was stored away in an

> equipment locker. All of his contacts were either out of town or unavailable. However, if he could get to a church on the outskirts of Mesa for Sunday worship, they would be able to get him where he needed to be.
>
> The young man had been staying in a local motel until he ran out of cash. Then he started walking the streets aimlessly and finally ended up at the sports bar. He couldn't even pay for the coffee he was drinking. In desperation, he picked up the phone book, looked up churches, and called our church because the ad appealed to him: "A friendly church that cares."
>
> After talking with him a while, I prayed and thought briefly about it, then decided that his story could be plausible. So I decided to put him up in a motel for the weekend and provide for his meals. During the drive to the motel, he talked about his experiences with Christ and how much his Walk to Emmaus weekend meant to him. He also expressed the hope that I would have the same type of experience in my life.
>
> I completely forgot about this stranger until several months later. I had decided to attend a Walk to Emmaus weekend. During that weekend, I woke up in the middle of the night with a start and realized that the decision wasn't mine alone. Christ had sent a messenger with an invitation!
>
> Were these events coincidental, or did God specifically plan them?
>
> I have never been able to confirm any aspects of this young man's story. I never saw or heard from him again. Isn't God truly amazing? Just when we think we are ministering to someone, we come face-to-face with the greatest evangelist of all, our Lord and Savior Jesus Christ or his messenger.[1]

I completely forgot his name until several years later when a fellow student at George Fox Seminary, W. David Phillips, posted a blog entry about meeting a person named James Finlayson.[2] His account sounded eerily similar to what I had written. I then realized that my messenger was James Finlayson. Finlayson traveled as a vagabond, defrauding churches for food, lodging, and financial support. He served jail time for his activities on several occasions.

1. Stewart, "The Messenger."

2. Phillips, "The Story of James Finlayson, July 11, 2006," and a sequel in Phillips, "The End of the James Finlayson Story. . . For Now, April 10, 2009."

I was the victim of Finlayson's swindle, but Christ transformed the con into a blessing. The small price I paid was much less than the benefit I received from attending the Walk to Emmaus. That retreat started me on the path to reconciliation and forgiveness of my father that I desperately needed. I could not move ahead until I resolved those issues, and I was the one who needed to start the process. I had become so afraid of repeating his mistakes and shortcomings that inaction paralyzed me.

I began talking to Nate Holt, a second career pastor who had previously enjoyed a seventeen-year impressive and successful legal career as a trial attorney. His legal profession ended when alcoholism and professional misconduct resulted in his disbarment. After having his main source of internal meaning removed, he turned to Christ in desperation. Christ rebuilt his life and Nate felt called to a preaching ministry, entering seminary when he was forty-six.

Nate was the first person that I knew well who transitioned later in life from a business occupation to serving effectively in a full-time church setting. On several occasions, I asked him about the transition process and the comparison between the two phases of his life. I finally became convinced that some form of transition was possible for me too. I asked if he missed being an attorney. He replied, "No, not really. I miss the excitement of the courtroom during trials, but what I have experienced now far exceeds whatever I did before."[3]

I knew I needed to be doing something beyond being active in my suburban church, and for some reason prison ministry intrigued me. I am not sure why; I did not have any close relatives that served time or any other tie I know of. I just know that somehow the Holy Spirit prompted me to go that direction.

When I first entered a prison for ministry over ten years ago, I did not know what to expect. Upon arriving at the gate, officers directed us to remove our belts, keys, change, and shoes. Each of us then walked through a metal detector similar to the ones at airports. If we came through the detector without beeping, they told us to wait while they opened a sliding set of bars. The signs above the entryway reminded me of the one at the gates of Hell in Dante's *Inferno*: "Abandon hope, all ye who enter here." After we walked past the first set of bars, they closed behind us, trapping us in a small corridor. "What did I get myself into?"

3. I lost a good friend and mentor when Nate Holt passed away in 2009.

was my thought. Then they opened the inner set of bars and we walked into the prison complex.

All prisons have a rank odor, an amalgam of disinfectant, strong soaps, and the body odor of fear. The concrete block walls and corridors accentuate the noise of so many inmates in close proximity to each other. Each inmate has on the same clothes as all the others so I was in a sea of orange, black and white stripes, tan, or blue.

Somehow, I made it through the first worship service and I did not feel nearly as claustrophobic on the way out. As I continued to minister in other services, I found that I was receiving much more than I was giving. Many of the people incarcerated had few if any visitors so they appreciated anyone who came to see them. They could be more open with us—we were not other inmates or officers. Many of them have the time to study scripture and bring a profound reading that connects with fellow inmates.

Since then I have served in many different prison settings from the lowest security risk to the highest that are on permanent lockdown. I do not think anyone ever gets fully accustomed to the smell, the loud noises, the paranoia and mental illness, or the faces of those who have abandoned hope at the door. What makes it worthwhile is that we are not the first ones with the Gospel into the prison. Jesus Christ is always there before us; we merely open all our senses to encounter him. We seek Christ with the inmates, being astounded and saying "Amen!" when he shows up in the unexpected and darkest places. Christ takes the incarcerated on a journey of discovery showing immeasurable depths of his love for them. We who are in prison ministry receive a privilege by participating in these expeditions of discovery.

When I was attending Fuller, I embarked on a quest for ordination in the United Methodist denomination knowing that rejection was the most likely outcome. I was too conservative for the area convocation. On several occasions, some called me an "ignorant fundamentalist" while I would be a moderate in most areas of the country. My premonition was right; rejection was in my future.

My meetings with the ordination board were bizarre. I described myself as being Wesleyan. Like John Wesley, the founder of the Methodist church, I lean toward free will and discipleship growth. The board then asked me if I was more Wesleyan or Methodist. I still do not fully understand the question. Were they were expecting me to show more allegiance to the denomination than to Jesus Christ?

On another occasion, I described my prison ministry activities. One of the board members asked me in all seriousness, "What value do you see in those people?" The question shocked me. They did not want to hear accounts of Christ's transformation of inmates' hearts. They could not envision the human value of prison inmates. I know I frustrated the ordination board because I did not answer their questions in the way they expected or preferred.

Not too long after, my wife and I left the United Methodist church we had been attending. My wife was fired from her position at the church as it started a downhill slide, and the same week I was told bluntly that I would never be ordained in the United Methodist denomination. After a short gap in attendance, we started worshiping with a Free Methodist congregation and I initiated ordination discussions with the denomination.

During this time, my wife and I participated in two incredible mission trips to the Middle East. The tour did not resemble the typical Christian tourism junket that visits Israeli Christian pilgrimage sites on large tour buses. Instead, we met people in their homes, stayed several days in the West Bank, met Iraqi refugees in Amman, Jordan, and supported Arab Christian businesses whenever possible. One pastor from the West Bank told us, "We see the people on the tour buses. They wave at us so we know they are Christians. Then they leave. But you didn't leave, you stayed." Because of these trips, I later traveled into Egypt, meeting more refugees and seeing how Christian witness worked in the Garbage City slum of Cairo. Also during that same trip, I traveled further down into Africa investigating support for an underground church plant. Those trips drastically broadened my outlook and understanding of the global church.

Meanwhile a friend of mine in the United Methodist denomination who also attended Fuller moved over to the same Free Methodist congregation. He planned to start a new church plant in an outlying area and I asked to join him.

We entered church planting underfunded, without counsel of experienced planters, assuming "if we build it, they will come." The initial worship meetings started out well, and we quickly grew to thirty people. The challenges came when we moved from a low rent storefront to a more costly local school. We did not grow and the setup and teardown effort was so draining that we had no energy left to connect with people. We were always short of funds and the increased rent eradicated other activities. We also found how challenging it was to grow an exurban church in a bedroom community. Every weekend, church signs filled the major road intersections. Every church plant was seeking people to attend their services, and most of the church plants traded the same people back and forth.

I had no plans to continue schooling. I met a recruiter for the George Fox Doctor of Ministry program at a conference. We talked about the possibilities and I became much more interested when I heard that Len Sweet, one of the most far-sighted Christian thinkers of our era, was the lead professor. After seeking counsel from trusted friends, I enrolled in the program. The entire experience of the DMin program dramatically expanded my understanding of what it means to be a Christian.

While I was in my doctoral program and co-pastoring the church plant, the Free Methodist denomination in the area entered a time of severe financial stresses. Ultimately, our startup funding dried up and we stopped meeting three years after we started. That is the typical church plant life expectancy. I do not regret joining with the church plant, but I probably will skip repeating the experience. My thoughts return to Joe from the opening story from chapter 1, whose pastor missed seeing and knowing the very best parts of him.

So far, I have experienced a sometimes disillusioned, yet satisfying, scary and exhilarating passage following Christ. I have made huge mistakes along a journey that can be described as nothing other than wandering in the wilderness. I have experienced profound mercy and growth, leaving behind my earlier views on doctrine. I have found freedom in not worrying about how to please the hierarchy. I do not know what will happen next, and cannot predict what will show up in the next valley or mountaintop. I am still a sojourner looking to find a path to a far country. I constantly remind myself that I must follow and not attempt to lead; Christ does the leading. What I do know is that I have never fit cleanly in a propositional framework. It is much more fun getting to know new people who have gone down a different path. The boundaries often feel tight and I have played outside the lines. But I have never understood why or how that fit into the kingdom of God until I started this investigation as part of my DMin studies. I look forward to continual re-creation by Christ on the path ahead. Len Sweet's words reverberate in my mind again, "So what is Christianity? It is Christ. Nothing more, nothing less."[4]

Next, let's dive into the Bible seeing what it has to say about journey in the Old and New Testaments.

—For Reflection—

1. Think back through your major life events. How did you react to them? Describe how they became important parts of your own faith journey.
2. Do you have a sense of what might happen next?
3. How have life's "curve balls" changed your direction?

4. Sweet and Viola, *Jesus Manifesto*, xvi.

4

The Bible and Journey

Wilderness, as a reflection of the richness and beauty of the Creator, reminds us of untamable and unpredictable realities. Are we ready for this larger world, this universe that by its very character challenges us to open ourselves up to risk? What kinds of risks will the God of nature require of us? What will it cost us?

—Luci Shaw, *The Crime of Living Cautiously, Hearing God's Call to Adventure*

The Bible begins and ends in a garden. Humankind starts in the Garden of Eden (Gen 2.8). Revelation concludes with a vision of the new Jerusalem with "the river of the water of life, as clear as crystal, flowing down from the throne of God and the lamb down the middle of the great street of the city" (Rev 22:1–2). The biblical writers focus on a central theme of exiting bondage, deliverance, and re-creation back toward the garden through journey into God's promises. For example, God said to Moses: "Leave this place, you and the people you brought up out of Egypt, and go up to the land I promised on oath to Abraham, Isaac and Jacob" (Exod 33:1). The theme of deliverance and promise in Adam and Eve's exit from the garden (Gen 3:24) echoes throughout the Bible and concludes with the promise of a "new heaven and a new earth" (Rev 22:1). These promises involve journeys, and the faithful receive the promises only when they journey with God where he leads. People, regardless of their generation, socioeconomic position, location or any other factor must leave their comfort zones and follow God down unknown paths they cannot see to reach the promise of the New Jerusalem.

If we have a biblical understanding of spiritual journey, then we see a new and much less restrictive paradigm of church and spiritual growth. The narratives of the sojourners and pilgrims found in the Old and New Testaments illuminate how God asked them to leave their dwelling or their place of understanding and strike out, following God, seemingly without firm signposts and unclear outcomes. These accounts point the way to what it means to belong into the magnificent, diverse, and organic body of Christ.

God reveals himself in the act of journeying, and the Bible is the journey's narrative. Sometimes we think that if we just get through the hard parts of the journey, then we will see the blessing God has for us. We do not realize that the journey in itself is a blessing, and, in addition, the Promised Land is itself a journey rather than a static destination.

The Canaanite Tradition

Before we can fully understand the idea of journey and wilderness, we need to examine the environment in which God revealed himself to the Hebrew people so we can understand how fundamentally radical the concept of faith journeys and a single creator God were. The Hebrew people were monotheistic, worshiping only God the creator (Yahweh). In contrast, the Canaanite tribes around them were polytheistic, worshiping numerous gods. The Old Testament contains many accounts of the theological conflicts between the Hebrews and their neighbors. The contrast between the writings of the Canaanites and the biblical authors starkly illustrates the differences between the belief systems and the environment in which the Hebrews became a distinct people group with their own customs and practices.[1]

In the early 1930s, a cache of Canaanite texts was unearthed from Ras Shamra near the west coast of Syria containing major portions of the *Ugaritic Baal Cycle*. These writings contain stories about the primary god, Baal, and other deities in the Canaanite pantheon. The accounts help us understand the environment in which the Hebrews became a

1. Parker, *Ugaritic Narrative Poetry*, 81.

distinct people group. The word Baal refers to one of various Canaanite storm and fertility gods and means "owner," "lord," or "husband" in various Semitic dialects, and Baal functions as the "husband" of the earth.[2] Many references in the Old Testament use Baal as a term for the fertility lord or deity of a specific location related to non-Hebraic, non-monotheistic people groups.

One of the accounts in the Ugaritic Baal Cycle covers the conflict between Baal and Mot, the deity of the barren wilderness. In Canaanite thought, wilderness represents the underworld and Mot is the god of death. Mot causes the heat during the summer and drought by swallowing up Baal, who dies each summer in a place of hopelessness and returns to the underworld. The rain stops falling, the land dries up, and the crops die along with Baal. At the end of the Baal cycle, the chief of the gods, El, celebrates Baal's return from the wilderness death into the life of the fall and winter annual rains.

> *Mot:* I will send him [Baal] in a great pit in the Earth [Netherworld]. And you, take your clouds, your winds, your bolts, your rains . . . with you, Pidray, Daughter of Light, with you, Tallay, Daughter of Rain . . . and descend into Hell, the House of Freedom. Be counted among the inmates of Hell; and you will know, O god, that you are dead. (CAT 1.5 v 4–17)
>
> *El:* Baal is dead! What of the peoples? The Son of Dagan! What of the multitudes? After Baal I will descend into Hell. (CAT 1.6 i 6–8) Let the heavens rain oil, the wadis run with honey—Then I will know that Mightiest Baal lives, The Prince, Lord of the Earth is alive. (CAT 1.6 iii 6–9)[3]

The Ugaritic Baal Cycle is strongly agrarian. All activities occur with the seasons, and the concept of a journey that connects a person to a transcendent power, deity, or to an end destination is largely absent in the epic. The seasons and gods are cyclical, the gods are arbitrary, and additional knowledge does not result in a closer relationship to the gods. This cyclical view of existence was the dominant worldview in the ancient world, therefore, monotheistic Yahweism, or the worship of a personified God, the single creator God, was a radical departure from this type of thought.

2. Koehler et al., *Hebrew Aramaic Lexicon*, 142–143.

3. Parker, *Ugaritic Narrative Poetry*, 147–151.

The Dead Sea Scrolls

The Dead Sea Scrolls provide a snapshot of a post second temple Jewish community that rejected the concepts of journey and Hebraic wilderness. Paradoxically, they moved into the desert to avoid the perceived corruption of Jerusalem temple and priesthood. Khirbet Qumran was the location of a settlement near the northwest shore of the Dead Sea, associated with the people who produced the Dead Sea Scrolls discovered in caves on the hills above the settlement. Archaeological evidence suggests that some form of community existed at Qumran from approximately 150 BC to possibly as late as AD 74. Some of their writings suggest that community members saw themselves as the repository of the true Jewish path that followed the "Teacher of Righteousness" into the wilderness. The community judged the temple priests in Jerusalem as apostates and the entire temple hierarchy as corrupt. In response to this, the bulk of the settlement likely moved from Jerusalem to Qumran in the century preceding Jesus's birth.

The Teacher of Righteousness was a leader and rabbi in the tradition of Moses. The Qumranic *Pesher*, or commentary, on Habakkuk records, "Its interpretation concerns the Teacher of Righteousness, to whom God has made known all the mysteries of the words of his servants, the prophets."[4] In the wilderness, the community could engage in what the adherents considered true holiness and worship and be on the journey's right path. The community rule reflected the spirit of the wilderness experiences at Sinai, and the organization mimicked the desert organization of the tribes, attempting to recapture the spirit of the Hebrew people traveling in the desert away from Egypt:

"All the people shall enter in order, one after another, in thousands, hundreds, fifties and tens, so that each Israelite may know his standing in God's Community in conformity with an eternal plan."[5]

Most likely, the inhabitants of Qumran chose the community location above the Jordan River with the expectation that they would be the first to join the Messiah on his return as "the sons of Levi, the sons of Judah, and the sons of Benjamin, the exiled of the desert."[6] They believed the Messiah would come from Babylon, entering Jerusalem

4. Martinez and Tigchelaar, *The Dead Sea Scrolls*, vol. 1, 17 (1QPHab vii 4–5).
5. Ibid., 73 (1QS ii 21–23).
6. Ibid., 113 (1QM i 2).

to conquer and reclaim his rightful throne. Being the first to join the Messiah would grant the members of community leadership positions in the new order. Additionally they would be the ones to recapture the spirit of Mount Sinai and journey up the mountain with Moses and his surrogate the Qumran leader, the Teacher of Righteousness. They attempted to avoid the apostasy of the Hebrew people left below the mountain by creating a set of very formal rules. Any breach of those regulations resulted in severe punishment, frequently leading to expulsion from the community.

They sought to keep the community pure and holy so they might experience the blessings of God. This philosophy includes no concept of growth and change while traveling in a theological wilderness because the community was the *true guardian of right doctrine and practice*. Thus, growth and change were unnecessary.

The Old Testament writers embraced the idea of growth and change because those are key practices that bring us closer to God. The first five books of the Bible, the Pentateuch (*Torah*), contain multiple accounts of journey out of bondage, journey to a strange new land, journey away from trouble, and other journeys of faith. The next chapters explore sojourns and treks found in the Old Testament.

—For Reflection—

1. Have you been in a group that feared change and demanded precise responses? Share your experiences.
2. Read Genesis 2:4–16 and Revelation 22:1–5. Compare the descriptions of the two gardens. What are the similarities? Where are the differences?
3. Have you ever felt that life is arbitrary and the "gods" have no interest in you?

5

The Hebrew Tradition of Journey in the Old Testament

In contrast to the Canaanite and Qumran traditions, the Old Testament biblical witness shows how wilderness affected the Hebrew people deeply. Time in the wilderness was a metaphor and a vision of a faith journey.[1] The close proximity of wilderness to the land of Canaan constantly reminded the Hebrews of their heritage, how God turned their apparently aimless wanderings into deliverance.

God banished Adam and Eve from the paradise of the Garden of Eden into the unknown troubles of the outside world. Abraham left his home and traveled to an unknown land at God's urging. Joseph became the savior of his family and the Hebrew tribe through his sale as a slave to the Egyptians. Moses reluctantly led the Hebrew people back out of slavery in Egypt. Jonah ran from God, yet when he finally obeyed God, the city of Nineveh averted destruction. The Hebrew people endured exile in the foreign wilderness of Babylon and then led back by God into Jerusalem. In all these situations, God maintained control and provided guidance even though many of the people on the treks did not recognize God's presence. Like the people in these biblical accounts, we have a hard time recognizing the hand of God until we look back on the expedition into a far country.

The Hebrew tradition recognized two main views of the wilderness, and by implication, journey. The first was a negative view of wilderness as a place of scorpions, serpents, and thirst where demons and

1. Louth, *Wilderness of God*, 50–52.

evil spirits prevailed. Aaron sent the scapegoat away from the camp so it would carry the sins of the people into the void of a "solitary place" (Lev 16:20–22). Edom turned into wilderness because of her sins: "Thorns will overrun her citadels, nettles and brambles her strongholds. She will become a haunt for jackals, a home for owls" (Isa 34:13). Ezekiel viewed it as a place for a new winnowing and purging similar to the first journey through the wilderness (Ezek 20:33–39). Jesus commented about wilderness, "When an evil spirit comes out of a man, it goes through arid places seeking rest and does not find it" (Luke 11:24).

The second Hebraic view was the dominant one, considering wilderness as positive. For example, time in the wilderness in the Pentateuch was a "betrothal period" of journey that ended with the settlement of Canaan. Hosea spoke of Israel and quoted God:

> And now, here's what I'm going to do:
> I'm going to start all over again.
> I'm taking her back out into the wilderness
> where we had our first date, and I'll court her.
> I'll give her bouquets of roses.
> I'll turn Heartbreak Valley into Acres of Hope.
> She'll respond like she did as a young girl,
> those days when she was fresh out of Egypt. (Hos 2:14–15 MSG)

Hosea continued the metaphor later in the book showing how God rescues the people who come "trembling like birds from Egypt" (Hos 10:11). From Jeremiah, "I remember your youthful loyalty, our love as newlyweds. You stayed with me through the wilderness years, stuck with me through all the hard places" (Jer 2:2 MSG).

We grow in knowledge through all the hard places although we usually do not like the process of learning such lessons. As people, we would rather have the lessons handed to us in a form that is palatable and easy to digest. We do not want to pick out the leaves, twigs, pits, and stones in what we consume because paying attention to each morsel of what we eat is hard work. Why does seeking after God put us in such hard places or allow us to reach the same conclusion as the writer of Ecclesiastes, "Everything is meaningless" (Eccl 12:8)? "Now all is heard; here is the conclusion of the matter: Fear God and keep his commandments, for this is the whole duty of man" (Eccl 12:13).

—For Reflection—

1. Where are the hard places in your life?
2. Respond in your own way to "Everything is meaningless" (Eccl 12:8).
3. Look up the scripture references in this chapter. What do they mean in your life?

We can join faith expeditions by reading the stories of baby boomers and their trips through the landscapes of their lives. These stories, interwoven between the chapters, connect our present day lives with the rich traditions and faith of those who have gone before, giving us hope that God is still powerfully at work. These stories came from interviews I conducted, modeled after James Fowler's Faith Development theory.[2]

God works uniquely in each of us, and the common threads in the tapestries of people's lives connect us together in the community and handiwork of God. Some of these accounts illustrate people that persevered in the face of great obstacles. Others show richness of wisdom within apparently ordinary life. We find common threads in the tapestries woven by other people's lives; we recognize the handiwork of God and the commonality of community that all of us possess.

These narratives connect ancient and present times, echoing the sojourns of the prophets, Abraham, the exodus out of Egypt, Jesus Christ, Paul, and many others depicted in the biblical accounts. They resonate with the experiences of the desert fathers and mothers, and the medieval mystics. As you read the accounts, look for images of yourself and your friends in the accounts. The discussion questions following the stories let you continue the dialog with God and yourself, illuminating both unique and common patterns in the threads through baby boomers' lives.

Story: Joan Talbot

Joan Talbot was born in 1960 into a Navy family, the youngest of five children. They moved every few years whenever her father received a new assignment. When she was about nine, her mother and father started fighting and divorced when Joan was ten or eleven. The pain and deep disappointment in the divorce still affects Joan's relationships today.

Her mother re-married and all the children moved in with their father, except Joan who stayed with her mother and her stepsister. Adding to the challenges, her mother became an

2. See the Appendix for the questions used in the Faith Development interviews. The names used in all stories are disguised.

alcoholic. Subsequently Joan spent the school year with her mother and the summer with her father. At thirteen, she accepted Christ at a youth camp, but found keeping her faith difficult while living with alcoholic parents.

She married her first husband at nineteen and they had five children together. She became "heavily involved in church until our pastor left his wife." Because of the pastor's actions, the church closed. After some searching, Joan and her first husband found another one. At the new church, Joan met her current husband, Ward . . . while still married to her first husband. Joan and Ward started having an affair, and eventually the two couples involved divorced. After the divorce, Joan and Ward married and later their ex-spouses married each other.

Joan described what happened during their time of adultery and turmoil: "At that time, we weren't going to church, because of the shame of what we did. That's when Satan knew where he could get me and his plans worked. . . . When Ward and I married, we started going to church. I felt like everybody was looking at me [while I underwent] shame and guilt. I asked God's forgiveness. I knew God forgave me, but I just didn't know how to forgive myself. We kept going to different churches."

A few years later Joan lost one of her teenage sons in an automobile accident:

> In 2001, my fourteen-year-old son was killed in a car accident. That was very difficult. I started blaming myself. It was my fault, because it was my punishment from God for the adultery. It was hard to go to church again. . . . About a year after the accident, the ambulance driver at the accident scene contacted us. He met with us and shared how that accident brought him to the Lord. He knew that they were Christians because a Bible flew out of the car and it was open [lying on the road]. Coincidental circumstances in his own life with this accident convinced him that God was calling him to come back.

This profound encounter transformed the life trajectory of Joan and Ward. As a result, they decided to try church again. Joan felt comfortable enough to share the story of her adultery. "*How do I forgive myself?* was a big question I had. Then the pastor's mother met with me. I remember her telling me, 'How dare you not forgive yourself!' I looked at her and thought, 'Really?' She said, 'If Jesus, who is the Son of God, God of the universe, can forgive you, you have no right not to forgive yourself because you are not greater than God.' Ever since that day, I felt totally set free. That was a big impact on my life."

A few years later, they moved to an adjacent state when Ward received an attractive job offer. The employment offer expired quickly, so they made a fast decision to move and eliminate many of their financial pressures. Joan had to leave one of her children behind with the child's father since the courts would not approve the child's move on such short notice. Still, Joan comments looking back on the events of the past, "God has totally changed our lives in this past six years that we've been here. I feel just so close to God and so much growth, mainly in my husband too."

Joan has undergone significant journey already, but in some areas, she is still in the beginning phases, most likely in Fowler's Stage 3. She looks internally at her own actions and responses as reasons for events occurring, when many are not under her control.

—For Reflection—

1. How often do we as baby boomers and members of other generations want to assume all our problems are fully under our own control?
2. Do we really believe Christ can transform us?
3. Do we act as if his power is limited? Why or why not?

6

Abraham the Sojourner

The story of Abram (Abraham) begins abruptly in Genesis 11:10 with a statement of his genealogy. In the opening verse of chapter 12, God asks Abram to leave his people, household, and country to journey toward Canaan. The account does not provide a narrative interplay usually found with other instances of divine call such as seen in Isa 6:1–13, Jer 1:1–10, Exod 3:1–4:17, and Judg 6:7–24. The text simply states, "So Abram left" (Gen 12:4). Abram continues to wander in Canaan as a Bedouin-like tribal chieftain in a difficult environment. The text provides no insight into Abram's view of God at this time but records that he listened to God and built altars. His later interactions with God suggest he did not fully believe God earlier in his life, and his motivations for moving to Canaan remain unclear.

Pharaoh took Abram's wife, Sarai, into his harem when Abram journeyed to Egypt, moving the tribe there to escape a famine (Gen 12:10–20). Abram did not tell Pharaoh that Sarai was his wife and half-sister. Abram did not lie outright, but he assumed the interests of the tribe outweighed the necessity of telling the complete truth. Pharaoh recognized that Sarai was Abram's wife and sent her back.

Genesis 20 records a similar event after God changed the couple's names to Abraham and Sarah. After another of Abraham's journeys, Abimelech, king of Gerar, took Sarah into his harem. He returned her untouched when he learned Sarah was Abraham's wife. In both harem incidents, Abraham's moral code fell short of the rulers' moral codes (Gen 12:18–19, 20:9). The text strongly implies that Abraham did not fully believe and trust God, and Abraham laughed at God when God told him about his forthcoming son: "Abraham fell flat on his face. And then he laughed, thinking, 'Can a hundred-year-old man father a son? And can Sarah, at ninety years, have a baby?'" (Gen 17:17 MSG).

Abraham already had a son, Ishmael, who had the right of a first-born: "Recovering, Abraham said to God, 'Oh, keep Ishmael alive and well before you!'" (Gen 17:18 MSG). Abraham did not believe even a deity could give him a son through Sarah, and she too laughed when she heard the news (Gen 18:12).

Abraham experienced personal challenges as a tribal patriarch. For example, Abraham let his nephew, Lot keep the better land on the Jordan River plain when they parted ways. Abraham rescued Lot when Lot became a slave of war and lived in Sodom, Lot's new hometown (Gen 14). God told Abraham about the pending destruction of Sodom and Gomorrah (Gen 18:17–21). Abraham's bargaining with God, however, did not reflect a chieftain protecting his tribe, but rather a philosopher who argued the rightness of divine punishment (Gen 18:23–32). Abraham never raised the issue of Lot and his family during this discussion.

To this point, Abraham had not behaved like the father of nations and a leader of even his own family as they trekked under God's direction. He distrusted God to give him a son and placed his faith in his own backup plan with his first son, Ishmael (Gen 16:1–4). If God could not deliver on the promises, then Abraham himself would ensure the fulfillment of the promises. Abraham believed that he would be the father of nations as promised by God, but his actions strongly suggested he would become the father through a combination of God's power and Abraham's personal efforts.

God tested Abraham greatly after the birth of Abraham's son Isaac (Gen 21:2). God asked Abraham to journey to a mountain and sacrifice Isaac (Gen 22:2), but Isaac was the son of promise through whom Abraham would become the father of nations. Ishmael had left home, and Abraham's hope rested in Isaac.

Child sacrifice was common in the surrounding cultures, and scriptural evidence suggests that such sacrifices occurred in Hebraic culture: "Shall I offer my firstborn for my transgression, the fruit of my body for the sin of my soul? He has showed you, O man, what is good. And what does the LORD require of you? To act justly and to love mercy and to walk humbly with your God" (Mic 6:7–8). If child sacrifice were required, the Hebrew God might become just another god in the Canaanite pantheon. Until God provided the ram for sacrifice (Gen 22:12), the story outcome was unclear and could have resulted in the effective demotion of God.

The dénouement of the relationship came when God said, "Now I know that you [Abraham] fear God, because you have not withheld from me your son, your only son" (Gen 22:12). Abraham's physical and faith expeditions slowly deepened his relationship with God. He embarked on a journey, stumbled repeatedly, and did not live up to his roles as husband, father, tribal chieftain, and father of nations. He showed that he did not fully trust God at first, and his internal and external conflicts interfered with his faith.

Abraham moved into faith through a journey. He did not experience faith's fullness until he relinquished everything willingly. He had to prove to himself, and possibly God, that he was willing to sacrifice the most precious thing in his life, the son he received when he was very old. For Abraham, faith was an extended trek with many twists and unexpected turns throughout life.

—For Reflection—

1. How does faith surprise you with twists and unexpected turns?
2. What internal and external conflicts interfere with following God?
3. Read Genesis 18:1–15. Most of us would likely react like Sarah, saying "no way!" Do you agree or not?
4. Are you willing to sacrifice the most precious thing in your life to follow Christ?

Story: Sharon Roman

Sometimes I use the expression, "What do you do when the wheels fall off?" You are driving down the road on your life path with no obstacles ahead and suddenly another car sideswipes you. That forces you over into a curb and the world suddenly enters slow motion. You barely get the car back under control when the back passenger side drops down violently. A horrible screech assaults your ears, your heart is racing faster than it ever has, and the car is spinning around in circles when one of your wheels goes whizzing past the windshield. After the car stops, you say to yourself "No, I'm not dead," but you are not sure why the car did not flip over. Life terrifies us when we are hit us with times when the wheels fall off. Sharon Roman knows about those times.

She was born in 1957, the third of four children. Sharon grew up in the south, "raised in a happy home with parents who were great role models." Her father was a minister and her mother worked in the medical records field. "I grew up with the church an integral part of my life. [It was] literally a playground because we lived in a parsonage. . . We played in the churchyard; we played inside the church. We were there every single Sunday. Even on vacations, we visited churches. It was very much routine for me."

Her father was a recovering alcoholic, and sober during most of her childhood with one startling wheel falling off exception.

> When I was sixteen, my father had a relapse. I walked into my house when my mother happened to be out of town. Suddenly, this man, who had always been a huge leader in Alcoholics Anonymous and had helped many other alcoholics over the years, was completely inebriated and passed out in bed. It was profound for me at the time, and very traumatic. It was also rough on my mother who was away on a business trip at a conference, and she had to come home when I called her in a panic. Ultimately, the change, in a way, was positive. It was negative at the time. It was a complete shock, and it shattered the image

> I had of my father. As I became mature, though, it made me realize that he was a human being, and he overcame the drinking. He continued sober for many years after that time when he drank. I think it ultimately showed me how someone can pick himself or herself up and go on, recovering from a traumatic episode like that.

After Sharon attended college, she married her first husband, and the results were earth shattering for her. All the wheels fell off at once.

> My first husband was mentally ill. He had his first nervous breakdown after we had only been married a few months. During that period, he became violent and he attacked me. Over the two years that we were married, he was ill off and on. . . I felt extremely hopeless. I truly believed, and still believe, that he couldn't help what happened to him. His brain was sick. It shook everything about my world because I had fully intended to spend my life with him. I promised for better or worse, in sickness and in health. Yet, I was literally in danger being around him, because I don't think he could control himself. I felt incredible guilt about leaving him. It's the only time in my life that I have felt physically ill from stress and from pain.

Her world shook again when her father died when Sharon was twenty-six, not long after he helped her through the divorce. As part of her further growth, she subsequently moved into a different role with her mother. "I still remember the first time when we were talking on the phone, and she slipped up and she called me her sister's name. It was a very casual thing, and then she did it occasionally after that. The first time she did it to me was profound because I saw it as a Freudian slip. She now saw me as more of an equal. I had passed from being a child to being an adult. I was still her daughter, but I was interacting with her as an adult."

Along the way, her understanding of Christian faith and belief transitioned from a rules-based version of faith into a more expansive conviction more accepting of the differences in how people approach life.

> In the church I attend now, the minister really challenges people to think about what faith truly means, and to think about what Christ wants you to be and to do. It's been an awakening for

> me. I've always believed [in God], but I don't know that I had a relationship with Christ before now. [Our minister] frequently talks about being open to accepting people where they are, and accepting the world around us and not judging. Again, that's different for me from what I've traditionally been used to thinking. It's freeing, because part of my belief was that you had to be good. My father was a minister in the same denomination. It wasn't really a hell fire and brimstone type of message, but there was still this feeling in my mind that you have to be good.

For Sharon, much of her wilderness time came early in life with her father's alcoholic relapse, the trauma of her first marriage, and the recognition of finite life spans for both of her parents. In all these cases, the events did not result from her choices. They were times of crying out to God asking, "Why did all the wheels fall off?" and receiving no answers or very unsatisfying answers. She is on further expeditions now, transitioning between Fowler's Stage 3 and Stage 4, mapping into a Reflexive Exile under Jamieson's scale. Sharon will likely frequently reassess the assumptions inherent in her beliefs for the near future.

—For Reflection—

1. Have you had a time, maybe health related, job related, or family related, when the wheels fell off in your life?
2. How much did it hurt?
3. Could you talk to God about it?

7

Out of Egypt[1]

The forty-year wilderness journey out of Egypt ended the Israelites' heritage of living under slavery, and during the journey, they encountered God in unexpected ways. Barbara Brown Taylor writes, "Much that is certain at the center is up for grabs in the wilderness, while much that is real in the wilderness turns out to be far too feral for the center."[2] *Salvation and relief came in the freedom of the wilderness outside the strictures of Egypt and city life.* God lived in a desert tabernacle when the Hebrew people wandered toward Canaan rather than a royal palace like the future Jerusalem temple. On one hand, disobeying God may have resulted in death in the barrenness, but on the other, obedience led to a continued journey toward a new life in the Promised Land.

Prior to their time in the wilderness, the Hebrew nation of slaves lived for 450 years in Egypt. Moses, the deliverer of the Hebrew people, grew up in Pharaoh's court. He fled to Midian and hid as a shepherd after he killed an overseer abusing one of the Hebrew slaves (Exod 2:15). The beginning of Moses's desert experience comes when he is in Midian tending his father-in-law's sheep at Mount Horeb.

> There the angel of the Lord appeared to him in flames of fire from within a bush. Moses saw that though the bush was on fire it did not burn up. So Moses thought, "I will go over and see

1. I am deeply indebted to Michael S. Moore for opening all my senses to the richness of the accounts of the Hebrews' flight from Egypt. He helped me understand how these accounts give us hope in today's world.

2. Taylor, *Leaving Church*, 172.

> this strange sight—why the bush does not burn up." When the LORD saw that he had gone over to look, God called to him from within the bush, "Moses! Moses!" And Moses said, "Here I am." "Do not come any closer," God said. "Take off your sandals, for the place where you are standing is holy ground." Then he said, "I am the God of your father, the God of Abraham, the God of Isaac and the God of Jacob." At this, Moses hid his face, because he was afraid to look at God. (Exod 3:2–6)

Moses recognized that he was in a holy place. He removed his sandals and tried to hide from God, knowing he had done wrong by murdering an Egyptian and then running away from the crime. God told Moses that he would be the person to return to Egypt and free the Hebrew slaves from their oppressors. Moses objected, saying he was not the right choice. When Moses asked, God told Moses his name. It is not a name of a god as found in the Near East, but rather it is the name of God who is—"I am who I am"—beyond any rational naming but the name of the one who creates (Exod 3:14). "The desert seems a fitting place for such a revelation: the desert, itself devoid of anything in terms of which any comparison might be made, the desert whose barrenness matches, by contrast, the transcendent fullness of God."[3]

After further argument, Moses journeyed to Egypt and told Pharaoh, "Let my people go, that they may hold a festival to me in the desert" (Exod 5:1). Pharaoh refused, possibly from fear that this action illustrated weakness or that the Egyptian economy depended on the slaves. Then God sent plagues on Egypt, violating civilized concepts since each plague was increasingly feral. Each plague pushed further away from cultural norms, approaching the norms of the wilderness. Journey became more and more likely when the death of the first-born spurred Pharaoh to free the slaves (Exod 12:31–32).

The journey of the Hebrews quickly became more difficult and terrifying, and Pharaoh's pursuing army trapped the Israelites against the Red Sea. Those events made no sense to the people: "It would have been better for us to serve the Egyptians than to die in the desert!" (Exod 14:10–12). God resolved the problem by parting the waters and drowning the pursuing army (Exod 13–14).

The Hebrew people expressed the same lament when they faced the possibility of starvation: "If only we had died by the LORD's hand in

3. Louth, *Wilderness of God*, 41.

Egypt! There we sat around pots of meat and ate all the food we wanted, but you have brought us out into this desert to starve this entire assembly to death" (Exod 16:3). God responded and provided manna for them in the uncertainty of the journey. The Hebrew people lacked food on their journey until God provided it.

God showed himself on Mount Sinai even more dramatically than he did when Moses first received the call from God.

> On the morning of the third day there was thunder and lightning, with a thick cloud over the mountain, and a very loud trumpet blast. Everyone in the camp trembled. Then Moses led the people out of the camp to meet with God, and they stood at the foot of the mountain. Mount Sinai was covered with smoke, because the LORD descended on it in fire. The smoke billowed up from it like smoke from a furnace, the whole mountain trembled violently, and the sound of the trumpet grew louder and louder. Then Moses spoke and the voice of God answered him. (Exod 19:16–19)

After this encounter, Moses received the Ten Commandments and the rest of the law. Except for one occasion in Exod 24:10–11, no one else could approach God face-to-face (Exod 33:11). The appearance of God frightened people, and would lead to panic if God came with smoke and lightning in a city or a populated area.

On the journey, through the wilderness God provided what the Hebrew people needed. He sent manna (a word meaning, literally, *what is it?*) for their food (Exod 16:31). He clearly provided other items as needed although not explicitly recorded in Exodus and Numbers. God had limits, however, for what he tolerated on the journey. God provided support during an extended wandering time, but he demanded the people's holiness and obedience as they explored faith. The Hebrew people tested those limits and experienced the consequences of crossing the boundary from holiness into apostasy: "The rabble with them began to crave other food, and again the Israelites started wailing and said, 'If only we had meat to eat! We remember the fish we ate in Egypt at no cost—also the cucumbers, melons, leeks, onions and garlic. But now we have lost our appetite; we never see anything but this manna!'" (Num 11:4–6)

God provided quail *on his terms*: "You will not eat it [meat] for just one day, or two days, or five, ten or twenty days, but for a whole month—until it comes out of your nostrils and you loathe it—because you have rejected the LORD, who is among you" (Num 11:19–20). God ensured that the people would remember their complaints and their questioning of his goodness: "The anger of the LORD burned against the people, and he struck them with a severe plague" (Num 11:33).

This same pattern of provision and questioning on the journey occurred when spies went out into Canaan to learn the condition of the land. Ten of them came back with tales of the Canaanites' strength and city fortifications. They reported the land flowed with "milk and honey, [but] all the people we saw there are of great size. . . . We seemed like grasshoppers in our own eyes, and we looked the same to them" (Num 13:32–33). Joshua and Caleb, two of the spies, disagreed and reported that the land was full of powerful cities, but "their protection is gone" (Num 14:10). Again, people sent their complaints to God: "If only we had died in Egypt! Or in this desert! Why is the LORD bringing us to this land only to let us fall by the sword? . . . We should choose a leader and go back to Egypt" (Num 14:2–4).

The people constantly questioned why they undertook this long and arduous journey when the local residents of the places they passed lived much better than they did. Moab was the source of great temptation. "While Israel was staying in Shittim, the men began to indulge in sexual immorality with Moabite women, who invited them to the sacrifices to their gods. The people ate and bowed down before these gods. So Israel joined in worshiping the Baal of Peor. And the LORD's anger burned against them" (Num 25:1–3).

God's remedy was drastic, demanding the death of those involved. When the leaders were "weeping at the entrance to the Tent of Meeting," a Hebrew man and his Midianite wife walked by. Apparently they had either just consummated the marriage or she had just moved into his household. The priest Phinehas immediately followed them and killed them, thus ensuring that the resulting punishment plague stopped at only 24,000 dead rather than wiping out the entire camp (Num 25:6–9). God praised their action. "The LORD said to Moses, 'Phinehas son of Eleazar, the son of Aaron, the priest, has turned my anger away from the Israelites; for he was as zealous as I am for my honor among them, so that in my zeal I did not put an end to them'" (Num 25:10–11). The vengeance continued. Moses issued strict instructions to kill the Midianite women, stopping the rest of the defilement (Num 31:13–24).

Other books of the Old Testament continue the condemnation. "They yoked themselves to the Baal of Peor and ate sacrifices offered to lifeless gods" (Ps 106:28). Hosea commented, "But when they came to Baal Peor, they consecrated themselves to that shameful idol and became as vile as the thing they loved" (Hos 9:10). Joshua wrote, "Was not the sin of Peor enough for us? Up to this very day we have not cleansed ourselves from that sin, even though a plague fell on the community of the LORD!" (Josh 22:17)

At first glance, parts of the book of Numbers seem to live up to its English name—a dull and dreary listing of census minutiae to gloss over getting to the "meat" of the Bible. However, a closer reading of the census information reveals a staggering difference. God commanded both censuses, and the respective texts read very similar. Contrasting the second census (Num 26) with the first census (Num 1) illustrates the devastating effects of Baal Peor and related events. "With their parents dying and Sinai fading from memory, the post-Sinai generation faces a difficult question. How can a weary, ragtag group of refugees *inherit* (Num 14:24) the Promised Land when Israel no longer exists (at least not in its earlier form at Sinai), and the Anakim, Amalekites, Hittites, Jebusites, Amorites, and Canaanites already populate the area? This question takes on new urgency with the publication of the second census in chapter 26. The new census list bears witness to the sad truth that the Sinai generation has rejected Yahweh's vision."[4]

The delay in the second census until after the Baal Peor episode showed that the remainder of the first generation Israelites who came from Egypt had already died, either from natural causes or the Baal Peor plague. "These are the ones counted by Moses and Eleazar the priest when they counted the Israelites on the plains of Moab by the Jordan across from Jericho. Not one of them was among those counted by Moses and Aaron the priest when they counted the Israelites in the Desert of Sinai. For the LORD had told those Israelites they would surely die in the desert, and not one of them was left except Caleb son of Jephunneh and Joshua son of Nun" (Num 26:63–65).

During the wandering, two main temptations faced the people of Israel First there was a temptation to stop and settle down, ignoring God's relentless call to "Go" (Gen 12:1–4; Deut 1:6–7, Matt 28:18–20). If the people had stopped while God's cloud and shadow continued

4. Moore, "Numbers," 194.

on, would God have continued to provide manna and other items the people needed? They underwent constant temptations to settle, stop journeying, and cease wandering. The journey occurred on God's timing, not the Hebrew people's timing.

Another temptation was the desire to retreat, to abandon the effort because it was too hard. The known character of slavery was better than unknown potential death in the desert (Exod 14:11–12). Even after seeing how God provided food for them, many still wanted to retreat. They preferred the gods of Egypt to the God of their fathers because they knew them, even though those gods were shams with phantom shadows. A human could manipulate the Egyptian gods, or their shadows, since they did not have life and could not interact with people. They could not ask a person to give up all they knew based on a promise not to the person, but their children and future generations. Those gods of Egypt might appear to demand sacrifices yet they did not strike people dead like the God of the Hebrews. Those gods were tame; God was (and is) feral, untamable. The challenges of the forty-year trek in the desert prepared the Hebrew people to enter the land of Canaan. They transitioned from a group of fearful slaves into a society who fulfilled God's promise to Abraham during their faith journey. They persevered, trusting the untamable God of the Hebrews who led them throughout their wilderness passage, even though they preferred the tame gods of Egypt. Like the Hebrew people, we discover on our quests that God provides signposts and sustenance when we least expect them. God leads us ahead, weaning us from the tame gods and idols of our younger years.

—For Reflection—

1. What are your tame gods that are easy to control?
2. Read Numbers 25. Why did God react so vehemently to the people worshiping Baal Peor? Bring that ahead to today's world. What in your own life resembles worshiping Baal Peor?
3. What enslaves you in your life?
4. Deep down, would you prefer the easy way of keeping the enslavement or do you want the hard way of trackless wilderness travel leading to deliverance?

Story: Lou Manning

The intersection of personal story and the scripture narratives connects us with people and God. We find meaning in the collision of the two, creating an amalgam that shows up how apparently mundane events become pregnant with meaning. We find our humanness in God, and we find the divine in daily activities.

Lou Manning was born in the northeast in 1957 and moved to South Florida with his family before junior high school. His family "didn't believe in talking about politics or religion," but he attended church as a high school student and encountered Christ profoundly during that time. He met his wife on a blind date while he was in college, and together they had nine children. Remarkably, Lou has a very stable employment situation in the high technology field, working for thirty-three years at the same company.

He has continuously served on leadership teams in evangelical churches, and has not experienced the disappointments and frustrations that lead to leaving churches. Lou's life and career path suggest low likelihood of a wilderness-type faith quest, but deeper inspection shows dramatic changes in his understanding of God. His journey started quietly. Between their third and fourth child, his wife challenged him to discover how God was calling them into child rearing. "We ended up deciding that God had called us to have children. That's why we had nine children." Each of their children had widely divergent personalities, which gave Lou and his wife major child rearing challenges.

Deaths within his family forcefully introduced Lou to his own mortality. "I've had a father and a sister that have both died. [My father died] from a heart attack. My sister was killed just after leaving my house in a head-on collision. Those two deaths were extremely profound learning experiences for me when I realized how fragile life was."

He and his wife also lost at least two children through miscarriages. "The last child we lost (their planned tenth child) was four months along. It was a very difficult time for us. I remember feeling the intense pain of losing a child, knowing what other people must feel. Even though we had nine other [children], I still experienced devastating pain and loss."

A few years ago, his pastor presented Lou with a radical idea. "The pastor . . . actually said he wanted me to stop reading my Bible, which I thought was a novel thing. I couldn't understand his reasoning very well. I was talking about how much we needed to be in God's presence and how hard I was working at finding it. I was taking personal pride in what I was doing." Lou was trying to please God rather than follow God and he finally understood the pastor's point several years later.

Later he started working with a men's support group that encouraged participants to deal with serious issues in their lives. Lou's sense of meaning and understanding of faith matured after listening to them. "These men . . . went through way more in their lives such as loss of kids, sexual addictions, job losses, and other almost unbelievable situations. When I watched how they experienced and how they sought assurance that God loved them, it really changed me. My self-image [morphed] and I realized I thought I was working to please God." Lou learned how to trust God much deeper, integrating accounts of personal struggle and triumph with scripture into a powerful amalgam, allowing him to follow God rather than try to please God.

Recently the ownership of Lou's employer changed which has jeopardized his job. "I wasn't thinking I'd be displaced by the changes, but I was almost terminated. It made me realize that I was putting too much value in my position and in my career rather than how I identified myself with Christ. It gave me a realization that I need to live life for Christ and not just for myself. That was a tremendous life lesson."

Lou's faith journey has led him to a place that, on the surface, looks similar to his faith as a young person, but on a deeper level, he has matured dramatically into a Jamieson Transitional Explorer and into Fowler's Stage 4. His wilderness time has unfolded slowly with God revealing himself through personal losses, employment changes, and better understandings of how people encounter God through stories. "I think in terms of life, the stories make me realize that God is the giver of life. While we might think we have control over life, we really don't. I think that was the realization I came to on the life issues."

—For Reflection—

1. Even when we work hard at planning our lives, do we have control, or is the control in God's hands?
2. Deep down, do we like giving up control or do we secretly want it back?
3. Have you encountered Christ's transformation through strife and loss?

8

Is My Arm Too Short?

In the book of Isaiah, the southern kingdom of Judah is a conquered land and the people are in Babylon. Jerusalem was a heap of rubble with no king, no commerce, and no pilgrims (Isa 34:8–15). However even in the destruction, hope is not lost and the Hebrew people look forward to restoration: Mountains became level, the valleys filled in, and the rugged places smoothed:

> A voice of one calling:
> "In the desert prepare
> the way for the Lord;
> make straight in the wilderness
> a highway for our God.
> Every valley shall be raised up,
> every mountain and hill made low;
> the rough ground shall become level,
> the rugged places a plain.
> And the glory of the Lord will be revealed,
> and all mankind together will see it. For the mouth of the
> Lord has spoken." (Isa 40:3–5)

This passage, quoted in Matt 3:3, Mark 1:2–3, Luke 3:4–6, and John 1:23 referring to John the Baptist, formed the introduction to the extended wilderness symbolism in Isaiah 40—55. For examples, see Isa 41:17–20, 43:19–21, 48:20–21, 49:8–12, and 55:12–13.

When the time came to leave Babylon and return to Jerusalem, God provided for them through the trial of the journey. He reminding the people how he provided water in the dry desert:

> Leave Babylon,
> flee from the Babylonians!
> Announce this with shouts of joy
> and proclaim it.
> Send it out to the ends of the earth;
> say, "The LORD has redeemed his servant Jacob."
> They did not thirst when he led them through the deserts;
> he made water flow for them from the rock;
> he split the rock
> and water gushed out. (Isa 48:20–21)

The Hebrew people in the Babylonian exile asked themselves if God was really for them or against them. They felt abandoned since they were slaves and not in their homeland. Did they really believe God's command to return to Jerusalem? Was God's arm (or hand) too short? Had he not abandoned them? Walter Brueggemann examines the core issues.

> For if Yahweh is willing and faithful, then perhaps Yahweh lacks power and is not sovereign. Thus in such an extreme case, Yahweh will defiantly say to exilic Israel. "Is my hand shortened, that it cannot redeem? Or have I no power to deliver?" (Isa 50:2). Yahweh's defiance suggests that this is a response to something that was voiced by exilic, doubting Israel, something that was wondered out loud—perhaps that Yahweh had a "short hand." Yahweh had, in the past, a "strong arm and outstretched hand" by which to rescue Israel. But that arm now does not seem strong, and the hand seems to have shriveled to irrelevance. Apparently, this was a charge made by Israel in exile. Yahweh vigorously refutes the charge, with the vociferousness of grammatically emphatic construction: "Is my hand indeed shortened?" The answer of Isa 50:2b–3 asserts Yahweh's enormous power. And in Isa 59:1 the same issue is raised with the same wording, but now in a resolving indicative statement that vindicates Yahweh and indicts Israel. Thus the suffering of Israel is brought back into the sensible framework of covenantal sanctions, so that the question of Yahweh's power is muted.[1]

The "strong arm and outstretched hand" of God was only apparent looking in retrospective. This is a frequent complaint of people on a faith journey. They know that they are moving into another place, but cannot see down the road since God has not chosen to reveal the

1. Brueggemann, *Theology*, 323.

outcome to them. Like the Hebrew people traveling back to Jerusalem, they question the need for such a difficult journey in dangerous areas.

—For Reflection—

1. Have you felt like God abandoned you during times in your life?
2. If the journey is so difficult and dangerous, then why do we need to try it?
3. What if God leaves us stranded in the middle of our travels?
4. Re-read Walter Brueggemann's quotation on page 62 and the Bible verses he references. Has God's arm ever seemed "too short" to offer help during your times of doubt and challenge?

Story: Will Branford

Painful childhoods can cause us to head out on our own, aimlessly wandering, just to do something different. We stop beating ourselves up with a stick and the pain goes away. Unfortunately, we often stop hitting ourselves with the stick only to replace it by hitting our big toe with a hammer. The hammer keeps the painful stick away, and we think our life is better. The real healing and vanquished pain comes when we finally give the hammer to Christ and do not look for a substitute.

Will Branford grew up in a middle class family in the southern United States, the child of a traveling sales representative father and a special needs teacher mother. The family was nominally Catholic, and Will says that when he was twelve years old, "I pretty much got sidetracked," engaging in undesirable teenage behaviors. He and his father constantly argued during this time. Since his father was only home on weekends, Will received a whipping each Friday night for apparent misbehaviors during the week. What a major disconnect between the offense and the punishment! He even dreamed about killing his father: "I really had that much hate for my father at the time."

He discovered, or possibly rediscovered Christ at seventeen. "It was pretty miraculous to me. For the first time in my life, I could read out of the Bible and just totally understand it. There's something about being in the grace of God and reading his word, because it all makes sense." Will's understanding of the Bible was typical of a seventeen year old who discovered it for the first time.

The effects of his conversion did not last very long, especially after he married his first wife:

> I turned my back on the Christian life, ended up getting divorced and just going wild. From there I spent probably thirty years of drugs, drinking, and dealing. [I have] been busted three times. Through all that, I knew that God's presence was still there even though I had turned my back on him. He still had my back, because with the things that I did. I should have been dead. Even though I turned my back, he never turned his. He

> carried me through all that. I always knew I had to get back to a Christian life and a faith.

During this time of wilderness wandering, God's voice or touch seemed distant to Will, and he rarely thought about God. Will spent thirty years in the barren, thorn bush-filled wilderness looking for meaning and never finding it. He later recognized that God never abandoned him during his struggles. He compares God's love to that of parents: "No matter what I did, no matter what I put my parents through, they always loved me. They never gave up on me. And God doesn't give up on you."

A turning point in Will's departure from his relational wasteland occurred when his father was hospitalized for breaking his hip. The much-needed reconciliation left over from childhood finally commenced. Will comments,

> I spent eight days with my father in the hospital, twenty-four hours a day. I don't think that he ever thought I would do that. . . . There was a couple of times I told him [that] I love him. His response to that was, "I know you do." It wasn't, "I love you, too," or anything like that. I didn't expect anything else from him, but it hurt. After he got out of the hospital, he told me, "You'll never know how much I appreciate it. If I tried to let you know how much I appreciated it, I could never do it, until I die." That meant a lot to me.

As part of his faith journey, Will and his family now attend church. After being away from the church for thirty years, he understands staying connected with his Christian faith. "I've been married five times. When I married my present wife, I knew that if I was going to make the marriage last, I couldn't live the way I'd been living. Obviously, I'd been married four other times and divorced for a reason. That reason was the lifestyle that I led. With my new wife having a daughter, I knew that there was no way I was going to be the husband and father I had to be, without having God in my life."

Sometimes the wilderness and the escape from bondage teach us unexpected lessons. When asked what one thing he would change in his life, Will replied, "The thirty years I lost. It's a mixed emotions thing, because if I didn't do those thirty years, where would I be today? Would I be in the same place?

I have a wife and a daughter that I love with all my heart. Had I done those years differently, would I have the same things I have today?"

Will Branford gave up the stick and hammer after he decided to stop smashing his toes. In addition, he did not replace the hammer with anything else. He let Christ smash the hammer. His comments show he does not fit the traditional idea of a church attendee, nor would he be comfortable in many church environments. He lived "on the edge" for much of his adult life, and like Jacob, he recognizes God when he looks backward: "Surely the LORD is in this place, and I was not aware of it" (Gen 28:16). His understanding of God is much more personal because Will knows he could have died in many places in his wilderness wanderings. He also understands that his Christian faith journey is very dependent on Christ. Without God, his faith journey would have taken a different path. Will fits into Fowler's Stage 4 category and Jamieson's Transitional Explorer with some tendencies toward Fowler's Stage 5. He will likely continue to transition into different faith trajectories as the changes in his life unfold.

—For Reflection—

1. When have you hit your big toe with a spiritual hammer?
2. What would it take you to give the hammer to Christ so he can throw it out with the garbage of sin?
3. How can you trade the hammer in for Christ's message of grace? What does that look like at work, driving the kids to soccer, in the kitchen, relaxing in the evening, or in all the seemingly mundane parts of your life?

9

Elijah and the Prophets of Baal

THE ACCOUNTS OF THE prophets contain numerous examples of journeys. For example, the stories of Elijah present a dominant theme of conflict between Elijah and the kings of Israel over syncretistic Baal worship (1 Kings 17:19–21; 2 Kings 1–2). Elijah fled from Ahab after he told the about a forthcoming extended drought. Ravens fed Elijah during his wilderness journey and exile (1 Kings 17:4–6), and God told him to see Ahab again after three years in the wilderness although it was a dangerous act: "Is that you [Elijah], you troubler of Israel?" (1 Kings 18:17). Elijah challenged the 450 prophets of Baal to a contest on Mount Carmel (1 Kings 18:20–22) and Elijah rebuilt an old altar in the middle of Baal's own high place after the successful contest.

The narrative passages in 1 Kings contain one of the most biting satirical interactions in the Old Testament. When the Baal prophets could not call down fire on their altar, Elijah taunted them and said, "Shout louder." Elijah suggested their god, Baal, was drunk and sleeping off a hangover, or possibly stuck in the latrine (1 Kings 18:27). After dousing God's altar with water, which was a profligate waste during a time of severe drought, Elijah called on God: "Answer me, O LORD, answer me, so these people will know that you, O LORD, are God, and that you are turning their hearts back again" (1 Kings 18:37). God consumed the altar with fire (1 Kings 18:38).

Elijah fled quickly because the crowd killed the prophets of Baal, and Ahab's wife Jezebel swore an oath to kill Elijah (1 Kings 19:2). The biblical writer records, "Elijah was afraid and ran for his life" (1 Kings 19:3). He journeyed to the desert and cried out to God, "I have had enough, Lord. . . . Take my life; I am no better than my ancestors" (1 Kings 19:4). After Elijah slept and ate what God provided, Elijah was still afraid for his life: "I am the only one left, and now they are trying to kill me too" (1 Kings 19:10).

Next, God promised that he would pass by and Elijah would see him (1 Kings 19:11). God was not in the wind, or the earthquake or the fire; God was in the "gentle whisper" that followed (1 Kings 19:12). Even though Elijah had largely defeated the forces of Baal, he needed encouragement to understand God was still with him.

Elijah lived his faith in a journey. He battled depression constantly and appeared to dislike the role of prophet (1 Kings 19:3–4, 19:14). Constantly afraid for his life, he survived those in Israel trying to kill him because God sustained him through all his passages and adventures. The excursion experiences transformed Elijah and fulfilled God's plan, even when Elijah was afraid that God would not protect him. God never abandoned Elijah even when he questioned his own ability to continue.

—For Reflection—

1. We all have Baals and other false gods in our lives that distract us from the one true God. What are some of your Baals?
2. Read 1 Kings 19:1–7. Has God given you strength when all you wanted to do was give up?
3. Have you experienced God as an earthquake or fire? Have you experienced him as a gentle whisper?

Story: Brandon Howard

Irony is a major element in major triumphs and tragedies. How many times does the outcome of a major military conflict hinge on minor errors, the uncertainty of weather, accidental discovery of the opponent's plans, or similar apparently unrelated factors. Sometimes Christ's grace is ironic in the face of major health obstacles.

Brandon Howard is the oldest of six children, and as a child attended twenty-three different schools since his family moved frequently. He found stability by joining the Air Force after he graduated from high school, and retired after twenty years of service. While he was in the Air Force, Brandon and his wife raised their two biological children whom are now grown and living on their own.

Not long after he left the Air Force, Brandon and his wife attended a presentation at their church about an urgent need for foster parents. He was unemployed at the time, so the two decided to attend the mandatory training course. The state agency paid foster parents for a child's care, which would give his family greatly needed income. They accepted their first child, specializing in "medically fragile" children.

They fell completely in love with that first child and eventually adopted her. Brandon and his wife discovered they deeply enjoyed caring for these children, and continued to accept additional foster children with health challenges.

One child completely turned their world upside down. She breathed through a tracheotomy tube and otherwise did not have many health challenges. One night they put her to bed as usual and went back to their normal nighttime activities. Later Brandon went to the bedroom to check on her and found her completely blue. She had pulled out her tracheotomy tube and turned over, blocking the airway.

Brandon started CPR immediately and yelled at his wife to call 911. The paramedics arrived rapidly. He asked them if they wanted to take over the CPR. They responded, "No, you're doing fine. Keep it up."

The police and the state agency investigated and determined that all the events were accidental so the Howards could keep her under their foster care. The lack of oxygen caused brain and organ damage so the child had no conscious level responses. She began to recover and showed increasing signs of awareness over time, keeping hope alive in Brandon and his wife. They started the adoption process for her.

Their hope gave way to a devastating day four years later:

> For four years, we took care of her under the assumption that God was going to heal her. Then one day she died, unexpectedly. God healed her by taking her. He didn't heal her and let her continue to live. So we don't know God's plan. We don't know why we had to take care of her for four years with the assumption that she was going to live, when she could have died four years earlier. So it doesn't matter what we do, God does what God wants to do.

The profound irony and pain of the loss made its full impact a week later when they received final approval of their adoption petition. This tragedy profoundly affected Brandon and his family for many years. His wife could not pray for two years afterward; she blamed God for not taking care of the child. They went through such devastating distress that they vowed never to care for a tracheotomy child again. In a further ironic twist, they later accepted another tracheotomy baby, whom they have now adopted. They have additionally adopted another girl who suffers from shaken baby syndrome with resultant limited brain function.

Brandon looks back on the effect of her death: "I think having a death of a close one . . . has changed my perspective of life's meaning, because life only means as much you put into it. We're only going to be on this earth for so long. I think when people say, 'How are you', and their response is, 'Well I'm fine because I'm on this side of the dirt.' That's not what I strive for. I strive to be with the Lord, and if I'm on the other side of the dirt, then that means I'm with the Lord."

During the last two years, Brandon and his family moved from an evangelical to a Pentecostal worship style, which was a major transition. He used to worry if people were worthy to take communion, but he no longer asks that question. He comments, "I do not know the mind or heart of anybody who takes communion. I try not to be judgmental like I used to be. Instead of looking outwardly, I try to only look inwardly for myself."

Brandon matches most closely with Fowler's Stage 4 with some Stage 5 elements. Some aspects of his search for meaning match Jamieson's Reflexive Exile definition and others match a Transitional Explorer setting. His faith journey is continuing, and a significant factor in his trek is a continuing re-examination of his understanding of God in light of their child's death, and marveling at how Christ never abandoned them during the entire sojourn through their personal "valley of the shadow of death" (Ps 23:4).

—For Reflection—

1. Have you been through a personal "valley of the shadow of death" experience?
2. Have you seen friends go through such times?
3. Did the experience make you angry? Did it depress you?
4. What aspects were ironic?
5. Read Psalm 23 and imagine yourself in the Psalm. Are you still in the valley?

10

Running Away From Ninevah

The book of Jonah is a metaphor of running away, hiding, and reluctantly returning to God. Jonah was an unenthusiastic prophet who fled when God instructed him to travel to Ninevah and "preach against it" (Jonah 1:1). Instead, Jonah boarded a ship bound for Tarshish, probably located at the western edge of the Mediterranean Sea. Jonah headed away from Ninevah and attempted to place as much distance between him and Ninevah as possible. God sent calamities on the ship including a massive storm, and the sailors tossed Jonah overboard. God provided a great fish that swallowed Jonah, vomited him out, and saved his life. After Jonah returned home, God told him again to go to Ninevah. This time he obeyed and reluctantly traveled to the city (Jonah 3:1–3). Jonah, however, was unhappy because he perceived the Ninevites as evil and the enemies of the Hebrews. He told God, "It is better for me to die than to live" (Jonah 4:3), and he continued sulking until the conclusion of the book.

Two central themes emerge from Jonah's journey. Jonah's prayer while he was in the fish points to an essential truth: "Salvation comes from the Lord" (Jonah 2:9). God's grace allowed Jonah to try again and illustrates that journey is essential for faith. Jonah was a reluctant prophet and listened to God only after he realized his salvation was not under his control. Jonah may have refused to go to Ninevah without the experience of his first ship journey.

God stated the second theme, asking Jonah twice if Jonah had a right to be angry (Jonah 4:4, 4:9). God never fully answered Jonah since God decided the course of action independent of Jonah's opinion. God gave Jonah the task to save Ninevah, and the composition of the book of Jonah emphasizes the value of a faith journey. Jonah did not understand the full purpose of the journey just as believers do not understand the full purpose of their journeys.

Forrest Gump famously stated, "Life is like a box of chocolates, you never know what you're gonna get." The more we journey, the more we resonate with that sentiment and realize that we have very little control over the surprises on the trek.

—For Reflection—

1. As baby boomers and sojourners, do we have a right to be angry with God?
2. Do we blame God for a life that is not celebrity perfect?
3. When we don't know what is next, do we follow Christ or do we try to make our own way?
4. How does Forrest Gump's comment connect with Jonah? Is life "like a box of chocolates" for you?

We are about halfway through the stories, tracking through Fowler's Stages of Faith. Each one is unique; many delve into the hard places in life. Through all the pain, Christ appears alongside those on a journey, lifting them up when they could not walk on their own. Where do you see yourself in the narratives?

Story: Karen Carlisle

Recently I was in a restaurant with my wife. After we received our food, I looked across the dining area and saw a man with a Mohawk hairstyle. Today those are uncommon so I commented on the hair to my wife. The man was near the door so I figured we would get a closer look on the way out. After we stood up, I realized that I had fallen prey to an illusion. He did not have a Mohawk. There were two men sitting next to each other. The one closest to me had a shaved head and the one behind him had a full hairstyle. They combined to resemble a Mohawk from my vantage point. How often do we look at something and realize we are not seeing its true nature but rather a surface appearance or an illusion?

Sometimes we have a skewed view of reality even if we can see it clearly "right in front of us." This was true for Karen Carlisle. She grew up in the south, and her childhood was very challenging living with an abusive father and a compliant mother. She witnessed many unpleasant physical confrontations between them. Her father also aimed his wrath at Karen, "My father was very controlling and demanding, expecting perfection. Nothing I did was ever good enough." The family lived in a small town, so she experienced the rejection and isolation that came with the town's knowledge of the family situation. Karen comments, "It was just hell on earth growing up."

Growing up with strong Fundamentalist origins, Karen says, "My image of God when I was a child was hellfire and damnation. It was legalistic, follow the rules, and do exactly what you're told. God will punish you if you do wrong and he will have a reward for you when you do good. It was very legalistic." She left the Fundamentalist roots of her childhood, moving over into a traditional evangelical environment while attending college. Karen's growth into adulthood continued after graduation when she married her husband. He is her support and strength during difficult times. "He's been wonderful. I couldn't ask for a better man."

In recent years, Karen underwent increasing discontent that she describes as a "time in the wilderness." After her children reached adulthood, she enrolled in a well-known evangelical seminary seeking greater knowledge of God. A nagging sense of uneasiness with the western Christian church increased with each course session. "In the West religion has become business, it doesn't mean what it was intended to mean. It has become big business. It [currently] means form, structure and rules."

During this time of dislocation, Karen underwent a profound experience with the Holy Spirit. While attending a Christian weekend seminar in a remote tranquil setting, her world shattered with a night vision.

> The first night we were there, I woke up at two or three o'clock in the morning. I just woke up, just wide-awake. I had this profound sense of God's love. I got up and wandered around in the dark. I had an overcoming feeling of joy. All I could do was weep for joy. I sat and wept for a good thirty minutes, just joyous weeping. Seeing the beauty in things that were imperfect and I felt like God had made a profound revelation to me. I had never thought about things being imperfect as being so beautiful. It just felt like a revelation to me. I knew that evening that something was about to change in my life and God was asking me, "Are you ready? If you're not, you'd better get ready because it's coming." From that point on, an avalanche of things began to change in my life.

Part of Karen's course work at the seminary included an introduction to the Eastern Orthodox Church. "Initially iconography got me interested in the Eastern Church because I'm an artist by nature. Iconography is theology without words. I went a couple of times to [an Orthodox] service just because I needed to check it out." She has since united with an Orthodox congregation and is on the path to full membership in the church. "Eastern Orthodoxy is a religion of the whole person.

It engages every one of the senses and it speaks deeply to the spirit. I found a fullness there that I have not been able to find anywhere else. I felt like I had come home."

Karen's maturing through her faith journey time in the wilderness has led her to a much different theological place, moving out of evangelical practice into Orthodoxy. She more readily accepts the contradictions inherent in creation without resolving the contradictions. Possibly moving into Orthodoxy enables her to see more readily past the apparent Mohawk haircut and sense the true nature underneath with God leading her through the radical changes in her life as she moves from Fowler's Stage 4 to Stage 5, journeying from a Jamieson's Transitional Explorer to an Integrated Wayfinder.

—For Reflection—

1. When have you followed an illusion thinking it was real?
2. What helped you to move past the illusion into the reality of Christ?
3. Read John 1:43–51. When have you had a "come and see" experience?

11

Journey in the New Testament

THE JOURNEY CONCEPT IS a major component of the four gospels. They do not present an image of a hermit-like holy man in the desert, a temple-based priest, or even a discontented radical hiding from the authorities. The gospels certainly do not describe what we envision as a typical minister in America! Jesus and his disciples traveled frequently from Galilee to Jericho and then up to Jerusalem (Matt 20:17; Mark 10:32–33; Luke 6:17, 9:28–33, 13:22, 18:31; John 2:13, 5:1, 12:12). He even walked through Samaria, a journey that was anathema to most Jews of the time (Luke 9:52, 17:11; John 4:4–5). "The Jews answered him, 'Aren't we right in saying that you are a Samaritan and demon-possessed?'" (John 8:48)

The gospel writers also promoted a sense of constant motion. For example, Mark emphasized the journey aspect of Jesus's ministry by his grammar choices. He frequently connected sentences with the Greek word *kai* (and), creating a sense of anticipation by breathlessly introducing a new sentence.

In first century Palestine, Judaism was a temple-based religion. The vast majority of religious practices occurred within the Jerusalem temple or the synagogues in other towns, with very little worship or other practices outside those settings. Jesus, however, chose to meet people in their everyday settings, and he met them in the marketplaces, along the roads, in the synagogues, at parties, and other places where people gathered. Jesus met people outside the temple and synagogues, and he encouraged them to think in terms of journey because he encountered them where they were (Mark 10:23–24, 12:34; Luke 13:28 et al.). People did not have to meet the temple or synagogue standards to encounter him. Prostitutes, gentiles, tax collectors, drunkards, and the unclean were unwelcome in the temple, but they had life changing faith experiences after meeting him (Matt 8:5–13, 9:9–13, 11:16–19; Mark 14:3–9; Luke 19:1–9).

—For Reflection—

1. Have you had life-altering encounters with Christ when you least expect them?
2. How did you respond?
3. Read a chapter or two of Mark describing Jesus's ministries. Do you feel out of breath after you finished? Why or why not?

12

Jesus in the Wilderness

MATTHEW 4 ILLUSTRATES JESUS's journey in the wilderness at the start of his ministry after his baptism. Like the Israelites who spent forty years wandering, Jesus spent forty days and forty nights in the desert. His time in the wilderness recalled the journey of the Hebrew people out of Egypt and into Canaan. This echoing of the wilderness trek helps demonstrate faith as a journey. The Hebrew people failed at many points, yet God kept them as the chosen people (Josh 1:6–9). He winnowed out the first generation and those unwilling to follow him.

Jesus met Satan in the wilderness, and Satan offered Jesus shortcuts to accomplish Jesus's mission on earth: "After fasting forty days and forty nights, he was hungry. The tempter came to him and said, 'If you are the Son of God, tell these stones to become bread.' Jesus answered, 'It is written: 'Man does not live on bread alone, but on every word that comes from the mouth of God''' (Matt 4:2–4). Jesus quoted accounts of the Hebrews' wilderness journey after they escaped from Egypt. For example, "He humbled you, causing you to hunger and then feeding you with manna, which neither you nor your fathers had known, to teach you that man does not live on bread alone but on every word that comes from the mouth of the LORD" (Deut 8:3).

The second temptation scene placed Jesus on the top of the Jerusalem temple. Satan suggested Jesus throw himself off to prove God's love and mercy (Matt 4:5–6). Like the people in the desert, Jesus had to decide if he would risk God's wrath by forcing God's hand. Jesus knew God would save him, and he quoted Deuteronomy: "It is also written: 'Do not put the Lord your God to the test''' (Matt 4:7).

In the third temptation, Satan took Jesus to a high mountain and offered Jesus the world's kingdom and glory if Jesus worshipped Satan (Matt 4:8). Jesus could abolish hunger and injustice and make the world a better place for the price of his soul (Matt 4:9). Jesus quoted Deuteronomy for a third time: "Away from me, Satan! For it is written: 'Worship the Lord your God, and serve him only'" (Matt 4:10).

Satan's offers were tempting, and Jesus took them seriously. If Jesus had not faced true temptation in his wilderness journey, his testing would have simply highlighted the differences between sinful people and Jesus as a non-corporeal deity. The mention of manna in Matthew 4:4 would have made no sense if Jesus was only spirit, and not flesh. The temptations formed a necessary component in Jesus's character so that believers could have confidence in following him as they travel on their faith journeys.

Jesus chose to lay aside his divinity during his time in the wilderness and show his humanity. Since he was God, then he could just "conjure up" some tasty food (Kosher, of course) when he was hungry. Right? Not really—he turned off his first century cell phone and relied on the truth he knew from Scripture to sustain him.

—For Reflection—

1. What do we do when we face serious temptations in our lives?
2. How do we walk away from those things we know we should not do, but we really want to do them?
3. How do we recover when we give in to those temptations?
4. How do we respond when the ends are beneficial but the means are dishonest or distorted?

13

Traveling Through the Parables of Jesus

Jesus's parables describe faith as a journey, and he frequently used parables as a teaching tool to describe the kingdom of God. An English definition of *parable* refers to "a simple story used to illustrate a moral or spiritual lesson,"[1] but this does not capture the richness of the Gospel parables. In the biblical context, a parable is an extended metaphor with many levels of meanings. One single interpretation does not express the metaphor fully. Each reader and hearer connects with a portion of the parable that speaks into his or her life. The different levels and meanings contain elements of truth and meaning, just as a faith journey illumines truth and meaning in different aspects as the journey unfolds.

Journey is a prominent feature in many parables as characters in the parables encounter crises that force them to act. They change through the parable and become different people. For example, the merchant who found a pearl of great value sold everything to buy it (Matt 13:45–46). The persistent widow found justice through constant badgering of the unjust judge (Luke 18:1–8). Those who rejected the invitation to the wedding banquet regretted their decision, and those on the street were invited and rejoiced (Matt 22:1–14; Luke 14:15–24). The shepherd, who left the flock in danger, looking for a lost sheep, ignored the common wisdom and underwent a transformation when he found the lost sheep (Matt 18:12–14; Luke 15:1–7).

The parable of the lost son illustrated a faith journey from multiple viewpoints (Luke 15:11–32). The younger son demanded his

1. "parable," *Concise OED*.

inheritance from his father and risked the entire family's well-being because the son sought a luxurious life (Luke 15:12). The son returned from "a distant country" (Luke 15:13) after he squandered his inheritance and expected treatment like a hired servant (Luke 15:19). The father, however, welcomed the son and said, "He was lost and is found" (Luke 15:32).

The son underwent a faith excursion to the depths of Hell and back into grace, and his wanderings led back to his father who always loved him. Would the younger son have ever understood the depths of his father's love if he has not left home? Other characters in the parable underwent their own faith passages. The father accepted the son back and ran to meet him (Luke 15:20). Both actions were unacceptable responses in the Jewish culture of the time. The older son complained and sulked, but the father said, "Everything I have is yours" (Luke 15:31). The servants were uninvolved, but they reported the events to the older brother and witnessed the impact of the son's journey home (Luke 15:27). Christ is that father running to welcome us home after a difficult journey through the dark times with no light.

—For Reflection—

1. When do we think Christ has abandoned us?
2. When do we miss seeing Christ in our own time of darkness or running away?
3. Where do you see yourself in the story of the lost son? (Luke 15:11–32)

14

The Desert on the Way to the Cross

THE DESERT TIME APPEARED again in Gethsemane, on the Mount of Olives outside Jerusalem. It was the location of an oil press and likely surrounded by an olive grove. Jesus often went to Gethsemane with his disciples at night to rest and to pray after long days in Jerusalem (Luke 21:37, 22:39, John 18:2). It was not a literal desert being an olive grove and a favorite escape from the city. However, it became a desert again the night before his death.

> Then Jesus went with his disciples to a place called Gethsemane, and he said to them, "Sit here while I go over there and pray." He took Peter and the two sons of Zebedee along with him, and he began to be sorrowful and troubled. Then he said to them, "My soul is overwhelmed with sorrow to the point of death. Stay here and keep watch with me." Going a little farther, he fell with his face to the ground and prayed, "My Father, if it is possible, may this cup be taken from me. Yet not as I will, but as you will." Then he returned to his disciples and found them sleeping. "Could you men not keep watch with me for one hour?" he asked Peter. "Watch and pray so that you will not fall into temptation. The spirit is willing, but the body is weak." He went away a second time and prayed, "My Father, if it is not possible for this cup to be taken away unless I drink it, may your will be done." (Matt 26:36–42)

It was night and the disciples fell asleep. Jesus was alone, praying. He experienced the temptation of turning back toward Egypt and away from the cross that awaited him. Blood literally sweated off him as he thought about the journey he was about to finish. (Luke 22:44) Jesus accepted the cup, the fourth and final cup of blessing (*barakah*) of Passover that he would not drink until he was on the cross (John 19:28). Then he could say, "It is finished" (John 19:30), ending his last time in the wilderness.

—For Reflection—

1. When you think to yourself, "I'm glad that's over and finished," are you looking forward to what is ahead?
2. Or are you simply happy you can leave it behind?
3. Read Psalm 88. Ponder what it means to you.

15

Paul the Pilgrim

A PASTOR FRIEND OF mine shared what happened during a baptism at his church. The baptismal candidate had recently accepted Christ through a very dramatic and sudden encounter with the risen Christ. When the newly baptized man came out of the water, he yelled at the top of his lungs, "I'm so **** glad I've been saved!" All that I can do upon hearing this story is celebrate his enthusiasm and say "Amen!" for transformation and knowing that Christ loves him so much that he would continue to work on the fellow's colorful language.

When we undergo a dramatic conversion, how often do we instantaneously transform into a spiritually mature "ambassador for Christ"? Christ performs such instantaneous miracles when needed. "Jesus looked at them and said, 'With man this is impossible, but with God all things are possible'" (Matt 19:26). Even Paul, the most effective evangelist spreading the Gospel that the world has ever seen, did not instantly start announcing the message of salvation. God allowed him to process the implications of what happened while learning how to proclaim Christ's grace.

Acts 9 describes Paul's instantaneous conversion through a direct encounter with Jesus on the road to Damascus. Saul was transformed from a person who "was still breathing out murderous threats" (Acts 9:1) to "Paul," a dedicated follower of Christ. Paul commented, "Christ Jesus took hold of me," and he emphasized the instantaneous nature of his conversion (Phil 3:12). Blinded during the encounter on a journey, he regained his sight three days later in Damascus (Acts 9:18).

He shared his new understanding that "Jesus is the Son of God" (Acts 9:20) a few days later and shortly thereafter left Damascus: "I went immediately to Arabia and later returned to Damascus" (Gal 1:17). He stayed in Arabia three years before he traveled to Jerusalem (Gal 1:18). The Arabia mentioned in this passage is not the current Kingdom of Saudi Arabia, but rather the kingdom of Nabataea, centered on Petra.[1] He did not remain in quiet contemplation while in Arabia thinking about what happened to him on the journey to Damascus. Instead, he pursued an active ministry while in Arabia: "In Damascus the governor under King Aretas had the city of the Damascenes guarded in order to arrest me" (2 Cor 11:32). The king was ruler of the Nabataean kingdom, and Paul's reputation as a troublemaker probably preceded him. In addition, the Damascus Jews complained about him (Acts 9:23–25).

A life-changing crisis of faith completely rearranged Paul's thinking and his understanding of God (Gal 1:13–17). Paul's journey to Arabia gave him opportunity to think through the consequences and implications of Christ's message and to develop a greater understanding, but he did not engage in extended quiet contemplation on faith journeys. The people and cultures he encountered in his Arabian journey helped him define his faith and understanding of Jesus Christ and his message. The pattern of deepened faith and increased understanding continued throughout his life journey, travels, beatings, imprisonments, and conflicts with others.

—For Reflection—

1. When faced with dramatic changes in our lives, can we instantly process them? Do we need Christ leading us through the changes we will be undergoing?
2. When does Christ work dramatic changes and when do they happen slower?
3. Does the speed of change matter?

1. Bruce, *Paul*, 81.

Story: Peter Hobart

Each of us has our own journey to follow, and one person's journey is not identical to anyone else's journey. Sometimes we encounter journeys that on the surface seem to be staid, but deeper analysis shows they have similar cliff-hanging moments, times of placidly paddling down a slow river, and times of being utterly lost without God's direction.

Peter Hobart's journey started on the East Coast, where he grew up and attended church. He "wandered from the church a little bit" as an older teen. The police in his community decided some of the local teenagers needed a frightening lesson in humility. They found a group including Peter, brought them to the jail, and locked them up overnight. The next day the police freed them without charges, hoping the teens would not return to jail through their cliff-hanging ordeal. At the time, Peter saw it as small rapids in a placid river. However, if he continued down the same path, he envisioned a giant waterfall with jagged rocks that would dash him and his life to pieces. Apparently, the possibilities of larger and dangerous rapids prompted him in returning to active church attendance a few years later.

Compared to some of the other life stories included here, Peter's life has been a stable one. He met his wife in high school and they dated about four years before they married. They remain married and have two adult children and four grandchildren. He has not undergone as much turmoil in work, family, and faith as others.

Peter's faith journey underwent a transformation during a mission trip to Limón, Costa Rica, during the aftermath of the Nicaraguan Civil War. He joined the trip shortly before it left for Costa Rica, when another person dropped out. He reports, "We traveled to Costa Rica and worked with the Nicaraguan refugees. That was a particularly eye-opening time for seeing what the missionaries deal with in third-world countries, and that stays with you."

This trip was the first time Peter experienced another culture in depth, and he became acquainted with the local inhabitants. He grew significantly by being able to look at life and faith through the eyes of other people. Like many baby boomers that experience the dichotomy as transition generation members, he discovered that personal relationships meant more to him than accomplishing the assigned work goals of the trip. Peter recalls, "To me, just the fact of being there was important, but while we were there . . . we went out cold into the neighborhood. . . . They [Costa Ricans] were just so open to the gospel, more so than the people here in the United States. That impressed me a lot, that they were receptive to our efforts there. We were helping with the Bible school for the Nicaraguans, but I think we brought back more than we took there."

Peter is an example of a person who has not undergone major faith crises initiated by traumatic events in his life. He says, "I'm kind of unique in the fact that that I grew up in church, and my image of God has not changed. You know, the things I learned as a child have stayed with me. The relation to God has grown stronger over the years. . . . You make smarter decisions when you get older. . . . My relationship has gotten closer to God; it hasn't changed drastically."

Peter grew up in the church and found a stable faith in that environment. His family did not move during his childhood, and he enjoyed geographical and cultural stability during his formative years. After he became an adult, he moved several times in his occupation and sought stability in a local church. He and his wife are still friends with people they met through churches many years ago and remained in the same denomination for most of their adult lives. They thrived spiritually in that environment.

Peter has a mature faith (Fowler's Stage 4/5) but he is an exception to the typical Stages of Faith pattern of movement. He also does not fit in a specific location in Jamieson's scale. He received a deep faith early in life and it has not left him. His interactions with people while in Costa Rica gave him a "second naïveté," a time of looking over the edge of the cliff and having God's direction reaffirmed. He can accept paradox within a very traditional church environment.

—For Reflection—

1. When have you looked over the cliff into the abyss?
2. Could you see the bottom of the abyss or have you been to the bottom?
3. Do you look forward to the rapids ahead as exhilarating or are you concerned they are so large that you might drown or end up stranded on a rock?
4. When is the river of life placid and serene for you?

16

Desert Fathers and Mothers

Are you tired? Worn out? Burned out on religion? Come to me. Get away with me and you'll recover your life. I'll show you how to take a real rest. Walk with me and work with me—watch how I do it. Learn the unforced rhythms of grace. I won't lay anything heavy or ill-fitting on you. Keep company with me and you'll learn to live freely and lightly.

—Matthew 11:29–30 *The Message*

So far, we have voyaged with the people in the Old and New Testaments and observed how their faith journeys and struggles along the way parallel those in contemporary times as seen in the baby boomer stories. Frequently their radical encounters with God or their revolutionary actions took place outside institutional gatherings. Likely, your faith journey and struggles mirror the actions of the biblical characters or the accounts of boomer challenges and triumphs. Now we turn to the lives of saints who took a stand in the face of persecution and martyrdom, and those who sought to reclaim the vibrancy of the Christian faith after the persecution ceased.

The first recorded persecution of followers of the Way, or Christians, in the Roman Empire occurred in AD 64 when Nero blamed them for the great fire of Rome. Persecution occurred sporadically over the next two and a half centuries, particularly caused by their refusal to worship the Roman emperor as a god. The great persecution of

Diocletian (AD 303 to 311) led to Christians being tortured, starved, and condemned to gladiatorial sports to entertain spectators by their deaths.

What happens when Christianity and government merge into one entity? Does Christianity remain vibrant, offering the transformation that comes from Christ? Does it accommodate itself to the expediencies of the governmental environment and lose its fervor? Does Christianity flourish when it is openly practiced or does it flourish when adherents must meet in secret, facing persecution, torture, and death every day? Christians faced this question at the beginning of the fourth century when historic changes swept through the Roman Empire.

The emperor Constantine underwent a dramatic conversion in AD 312 at the battle of Milvan Bridge. He looked up and saw a cross of with the words, "Conquer by this!" Constantine ordered his troops to mark their shields with the Greek letters *Chi* and *Rho*, the first two Greek letters of Christ (Eusebius, *Life of Constantine*, 28—31). Constantine's troops prevailed, and Christianity became the official Roman religion.

The Christian religion became fashionable and a path to government service. Christians no longer met in secret under fear of arrest or torture, and being at home in the world supplanted the concept of being a wayfaring stranger passing through the world. Emperor Constantine's official toleration of Christianity implied a union between the soul and the body under the political state of the Roman Empire.

The tension created by Christianity's newly established legitimacy was one factor that precipitated a re-examination of the relationship between Christians, society, and government. Some Christians, called *desert fathers* or *desert mothers*, reacted to this tension by leaving civilization behind and moving into the desert as hermits focused on God. The dominant majority were men, with a few women also seeking the desert.

The desert fathers hoped for union with God through the search for nothingness in *apophatic theology*. Apophatic theology, or negative theology, does not attempt to define God within the limits of concepts and seeks God in nothingness.[1] The soul rejects all ideas or images of God and enters a darkness that is beyond understanding into union with God.

1. Lane, *Solace*, Kindle e-book, location 965.

The desert fathers believed language and other concepts describe God inadequately, and they sought God through their faith journeys in desolate places. They felt a kinship with Job and his friends by confronting the insurmountable challenges of defining the nature of God in words. Job finally realized that words were completely inadequate: "Then Job answered the LORD: 'I am unworthy—how can I reply to you? I put my hand over my mouth. I spoke once, but I have no answer—twice, but I will say no more'" (Job 40:3–5). The desert fathers let their existence speak their theology.

Many desert fathers lived in the Egyptian desert beginning about the third century and continuing until the fifth century. They left the ease of life in the Roman Empire or other civilized settings for profound isolation where they worshipped God without distraction. Hermits were most common in Lower Egypt. In the less remote parts of Upper Egypt, communities of brothers lived in semi-hermitic communities, and many extreme ascetics dwelled around Nitria and Scetis. Outside Egypt, some lived in the region of Petra in Arabia, Syria, or the Palestinian desert.

Most who chose the hermitic life came as young men, although a few women lived in the desert. They modeled their self-discipline after Jesus's fasting (Luke 4:1–13) or John the Baptist's lifestyle (Luke 3:1–18). They believed desert residency would remove them from the world, allow them to follow God's call, and keep their faith journey free of distractions.

Few of the desert fathers left writings, and most of the available information comes from sayings and anecdotes recorded by visitors or followers. The following examples of Anthony, Moses, and Sisoes demonstrate how some of the desert fathers viewed faith journeys as important parts of their devotion to God.

Anthony

Anthony, also known as Anthony the Great, was the best known of all the desert fathers. Born in AD 251, he moved to the desert about AD 285. His reputation attracted followers, and he became their spiritual father, or the precursor to a monastic abbot. Athanasius's book, *Life of Anthony*, became a primary factor in the birth of the monastic movement.

The following quote provides insight into Anthony's life:

> One day some old men came to see Abba Anthony. In the midst of them was Abba Joseph. Wanting to test them, the old man suggested a text from the Scriptures, and, beginning with the youngest, he asked them what it meant. Each gave his opinion as he was able. But to each one the old man said, "You have not understood it." Last of all he said to Abba Joseph, "How would you explain this saying?" and he replied, "I do not know." Then Abba Anthony said, "Indeed, Abba Joseph has found the way, for he has said, 'I do not know.'"[2]

The unknowing is a major step in a faith journey. Growth is impossible until individuals recognize they cannot understand from their own abilities and seek understanding from God. This frank acknowledgement of unknowing is remarkable considering the desert fathers had most of their days available for prayer, contemplation, and study of the Bible.

> The Lord was not forgetful of Anthony's struggle. God was at hand to assist him. So, looking up, Anthony saw the roof, as it were, opened, and a ray of light descended upon him. The demons suddenly vanished, and the pain of his body immediately ceased, and the building was calm again. Conscious of this grace, Anthony regained his breath and felt free from pain. He spoke to the vision that appeared to him, saying, "Lord, where were you? Why did you not appear at the beginning in order for me not to endure such pain?" And a voice came to Anthony, saying: "Anthony, I was here all the time; I simply waited to witness your fight. Now, since you have endured and not yielded, I shall be your assistance forever, and I shall make your name known everywhere." Having heard this, Anthony rose up and prayer, receiving such strength that he perceived he had never had more power in his body previously.[3]

God is always with us, but like Anthony, we may not recognize his presence until we look at the events in retrospective. Since God is present in the struggle when life events do not occur, as we desire, then like the Hebrew people traveling in the wilderness, we continue onward. We remain on our journey, on the road, in our cell either physical or mental, and continue in the darkness. Anthony and the other Desert Fathers

2. Ward, *Sayings*, 4.
3. Athanasius, *Life of Anthony*, Ch. 19.

and Mothers have earned authority because they traveled the same type of road. In many cases, their road was much more difficult. Challenges and wrestling with God are inevitable during the journey. Wrestling with God only occurs when he is close—God is always present on our expeditions even when we try to leave him behind.

Moses

Abba Moses was a freed slave who became a robber. On one occasion, Moses abandoned a robbery when barking dog sounded the alarm. He returned later intending to kill the dog's owner. Discovered again, Moses sought refuge from the local authorities with a group of monks in the desert near Alexandria. The monks made such an impression with their devotion and peace that he decided become a Christian. He moved into the desert outside Scetis where he lived as a hermit and became the spiritual leader of his fellow hermits in the area. At age seventy-five, he died at the hands of robbers after he invited them in.

"A brother came from Scetis to visit Abba Moses and asked him for a word. The old man said to him, 'Go, sit in your cell, and your cell will teach you everything.'" "Abba Moses said, 'The man who flees and lives in solitude is like a bunch of grapes ripened by the sun, but he who remains amongst men is like an unripe grape.'"[4] Like Anthony, Moses discovered that knowledge of God comes from God revealing himself rather that an individual's activity in the world. Teaching occurs in the everyday events and profound moments. He lived a life of patience, learning from the simple pleasures of deprivation and experiencing God in solitude, which is opposite to what the world usually expects.

Sisoes

Sisoes learned the desert way from another father named Or in Scetis. Sisoes left the area after Anthony died because he believed the area had become too popular. He moved to a mountain and lived there alone for seventy-two years. "Abba Sisoes said, 'Seek God, and do not seek where he dwells.'"[5] Sisoes seems to suggest that travelers should stay focused

4. Ibid., 139–140.

5. Ibid., 221.

on the destination; stay focused on Christ. Neither the dark nor the desert is full of demons, but any lapses in focus may cause believers to veer off course.

—For Reflection—

1. What do we learn from the desert fathers and mothers?
2. Can we reproduce their experiences in our own lives considering how busy we are?
3. If we as baby boomers are seriously considering retirement, is retirement a time to engage in more contemplation? Is it a time to take part in action? Is it a time to play golf, travel, etc.?

Story: Teresa Gentile

Is fear a motivator or does it glue our feet to the floor, preventing us from moving? Some fears are healthy. Fear of being hit by cars keeps us out of the street and safe. Fear of moving forward holds us back and may prevent us from receiving the grace in God's plans for us. If we listen to those in our lives who always say "no," are we moving toward God or are we trying to bar the door and cling to what we already know?

Teresa Gentile was born in 1950 to a military family, the third of four children. The family moved all over the world based on her father's duty assignments. They attended church faithfully at all the various military postings. Like a child frightened of the dark, she was terrified of God. "I was scared I was going to get zapped [by God] at any moment, because I was doing wrong things. I was choosing wrong paths and getting in trouble." She does not remember "hellfire and brimstone" messages in the base chapels and suspects her fear came from the discipline inherent in military families. Teresa matured as she moved into her teenage years, realizing "God was more about love and grace."

Teresa decided to pursue a career as a teacher when she was still in high school. She recognized an innermost desire in herself to connect with and assist others. While in college, she "felt like I had an encounter with God in the forest." God was calling her to pastoral ministry. At that time, very few women held pastoral positions in her denomination. Deciding that becoming a pastor was impractical, she resolved to be an active volunteer instead. She deferred God's call to the pastoral ministry until much later.

After college, Teresa married a fellow teacher. The first ten years of her marriage were good. Once they had children, it deteriorated. "I could no longer spend all my time focused on my husband. I had daughters who needed me. It was hard for him to share me." Teresa began marriage counseling, slowly learning how to make healthier choices in her life. Her husband refused counseling, because he said, "I'm just fine." The marriage entered a rapid decline at thirteen years. Her husband left shortly before their sixteenth anniversary. Looking back on the marriage, Teresa identifies the deepest depth of despair and fear of change in their relationship:

> If I were still married, I probably wouldn't be a pastor, because that was not a healthy relationship. . . He'd gotten to a point in his life when he became a hermit. He was abandoned when he was nine, and he repeated history. . . I remember one time in particular we had a fight. I don't recall what it was about, but we had had a fight and I had been put down again, told how worthless I was. . . I remember locking myself in the bathroom. My daughters were very young, probably maybe three and five, really little. I remember thinking, maybe they would be better off without me. Maybe I should just end it all. . . Then I thought, "My daughters would be stuck with their dad." It was that moment I realized how dumb it was and how selfish it was for me to think along those lines. I remember crying out to God and saying, "Lord, help me. I've got to do something."

Several years later after the marriage ended, Teresa received a diagnosis of virulent stage 3 breast cancer and the fear returned amplified many times over. "The oncologist said, 'Well, we'll do what we can to keep you here for five years.' It's scary to think that you might not be here to see your children graduate from high school." Miraculously the cancer subsided and she learned to embrace her fears, turning them into strengths. "The breast cancer was a time of joy because I knew God really did take care of me. The doctors certainly weren't optimistic that I would still be alive. I'm still here seventeen years later."

Teresa enrolled in an evangelical seminary to pursue her delayed call to the pastoral ministry. She attempted to balance class work, full time employment as a teacher, health limitations, volunteering at church, and raising her children as a single parent. Managing the multiple demands on her time was difficult; she continued on the path constantly making slow headway. Ten years after starting her studies, she retired from teaching to complete the ordination requirements for her denomination. "It took eleven and a half years to complete requirements [for the seminary degree] and graduate."

Teresa's journey continued and she has realized how much more she values relationships with people than she did in the past. She recently resigned from one church when the congregation was not able to pay her salary, and another church interviewed her for possible employment as their pastor. They asked her to serve as a short-term pulpit supply pastor, starting Teresa on another phase in her voyage of discovery.

One Sunday the new church did not need her since they had a previously scheduled guest speaker. That Sunday Teresa suffered greatly from "withdrawal symptoms." She comments, "I had grown to love them so much. It stunned me that I had developed such close relationships with them in a short time. I think God gave me the opportunity to fall in love with them early on so that would help me with my growth process." Shortly thereafter, the church decided to hire her as a longer-term interim pastor.

The longer-term offer tested Teresa. She came from a socially conservative theological background; the church is much more liberal. She has been going through the process of re-examining and modifying many of her positions, trying to discern the proper balance between relationships and doctrine. Relationships are becoming more and more important in her life as she moves through the paths that Christ points out to her.

Teresa has come to accept expeditions of discovery and lack of fear as a normal part of Christian faith, overcoming her doubts from her former husband's negative influences and worries from her health obstacles. She has overcome hurdles with God's direction rather than with her own abilities. Her growth in relationships illustrates the adventures and challenges of her life. She fits Jamieson's definition of an Integrated Wayfinder and Fowler's Stage 5.

—For Reflection—

1. As we look at our daily voyages of faith discovery, how many of our fears keep us safe?

2. How many of our fears keep us from what Christ wants to share with us? How do you overcome those fears?
3. Have you ever seriously contemplated taking your own life? What stopped you?

17

Medieval Mystics

For some people, combining "mystics" and "Christian" suggests a new-age type syncretism merging selected snippets of Christian faith and a self-based amorphous spirituality. I am not tying the two opposite belief systems together. Mysticism in a Christian context refers to the union or communion of a person's soul with God through heart-felt devotion rather than through study. Knowledge provides a starting point, but a person cannot begin to grasp the profound otherness and the majesty of God through book knowledge only. When baby boomers on a sojourn describe their dry times when they thought God was absent, they cry out in despair because they cannot find an answer through "head knowledge" or even in some form of words. When looking back on their extended Australian style "walkabout," they frequently describe encounters with God in the wilderness as occurring without words, much like the medieval mystics.

The medieval, or middle, era stretches from approximately the fifth century to the sixteenth century. A major event that initiated the era is either the end of Christian persecution in the Roman Empire, or alternately the breakup of the Roman Empire with the rise of small, localized feudal kingdoms. Together these events changed how the Christian movement interacted with the world and cultural milieu as Western Europe and the Middle East fragmented into disjointed pockets of civilization. The transition out of the medieval era into the modernist era occurred over several centuries. Gutenberg's invention of movable type and a printing press forced the end of the era within a century or so.

The medieval mystics did not seek God through increased knowledge, but sought to know him intuitively, beyond the rational mind. Their hearts yearned for God while their heads despaired of looking for God. Knowledge about God was insufficient, and union with God was the ultimate aim of their lives.

Later chapters examine the lives and writings of Julian of Norwich, Teresa of Ávila, and John of the Cross. They were medieval mystics whose lives exemplified spiritual journeys in the wilderness. Their writings contain some of the deepest and most profound insights concerning faith expeditions ever recorded. They have much to teach us as we seek answers but discover that finding the answers is not the ultimate goal. The trek itself, which connects us with God, is the point of our searching. The end of the rainbow after we finish our time in the wilderness is not the Promised Land. We have been roaming in the Promised Land found in the wilderness and like the disciples on the road to Emmaus, have not recognized Christ walking with us (Luke 24:13).

—For Reflection—

1. How is the wilderness like the Promised Land for you? If not, why not?
2. Read Luke 24:13-34. Have you ever walked alongside Christ and did not recognize him?

Story: Michelle Myers

How much of faith is a wrestling with God? Is the wrestling and struggle a rejection of authority or is it a way of understanding God better? Consider the base meaning of the name *Israel*. A literal translation of *Israel* is *he wrestles with God*, which is the name God gave Jacob after the two wrestled the entire night (Gen 32:22–31). Jacob grabbed the heel of his twin Esau when they were born, trying to be born first (Gen 25:24–26). Jacob persuaded Esau to giving up his birthright in exchange for some bread and lentil stew (Gen 25:29–34), and pretended to be his brother Esau to receive the firstborn blessing from their father Isaac (Gen 27). Hosea summarized the wrestling, "In the womb he grasped his brother's heel; as a man he struggled with God" (Hos 12:3).

Michelle Myers follows in the tradition of Jacob, wrestling with God and seeking to understand God further. She is an ordained pastor in one of the larger mainline denominations, and has always questioned authority and external control: "I'm anti-authority. I struggle with authority and with discipline and things like that. So that's defining of my personality, I think." Her mother was Catholic, and her father was an atheist. Born in Saudi Arabia, she remained there until she came to the United States in the ninth grade to attend a girls' boarding school.

Michelle's father "did not want us to be brainwashed" by Christian churches while she and her sister were growing up. Yet, she started on her faith journey early in life. Michelle comments,

> My first memory of God is a dream that I had when I was a very little girl. I dreamed I was walking across the desert. I walked over a sand dune and there was a little temple. I went into the temple and it was full of animals that were having a great party. The giraffe came up to me and said, "You should go into this room." There was a little room in the center of the temple. The giraffe said, "Go in, and you'll meet God." I walked into the room and woke up. [I had] some strange sense of the presence

of God, and there was something holy about God and special. God was joyful [and] it was a joyful kind of a setting. That was about all I knew.

The origins of faith began appearing, and Michelle continued to sense God was part of her life.

The next stage in Michelle's journey occurred after she left home. "I was fifteen, in boarding school, and away from my family for the first time. I had a kind of breakdown and the girls at the school introduced me to the Gospel. That was a huge turning point for me. . . . It was a simple sharing of the Gospel and not much more."

She met her husband, who was a Christian, a year after she finished college. Neither of them attended church until their first child was two years old, but Michelle wanted her children to have the church experience she missed. She and her husband started attending church and slowly became more active in church activities. After moving to her current state in 1991, she began to sense a call to ordained ministry and entered seminary about six years later. In the process, several friends and mentors helped increase her understanding of scripture and church history. Michelle comments, "That process [of understanding] continues today."

In the midst of these transitions, her family underwent very painful desert experiences with two disastrous church involvements. They joined a church shortly after the lead pastor left under undesirable circumstances. He later returned to the lead pastor position and most of the people attending left the next week and never came back. Michelle's family tried a new church plant. However, the plant failed in the transition from the entrepreneurial startup phase to a team-building phase. Michelle comments, "[The first non-startup] pastor turned out to be trouble. . . . It was a terrible, terrible situation for everybody. There were times . . . that I felt completely abandoned." Because of the turmoil and the devastating mental toll, her husband refused to become deeply involved in any other church. Her children have completely abandoned attending church.

Michelle, however, grew by a different path through this painful situation: "But through the process . . . I began to understand that it didn't matter what had happened. God had not left the building. But that was really painful, and that [wilderness time] lasted for at least two years of struggle."

Based on our conversation, Michelle's struggles with authority likely stemmed from the stormy relationship with her father. They argued frequently when she was growing up, and they did not grow much closer over the rest of his life. Her father passed away about three and a half years ago, and Michelle comments about their relationship: "I'd always wanted to have a good relationship [with my father], and didn't know how to make that happen. I continued to pray that God would help me to forgive. . . . [the relationship] would be healed, and somehow that would happen. One day I was in the shower and I was praying that prayer again because I was really struggling with my feelings for my father. Suddenly I felt completely at peace. I still regret that we didn't have a good relationship, but I feel like things are mended between us somehow." She learned how to deal with her father's death during this life transition, and she continued her faith voyage by wrestling with her internal emotions while wrestling with God. Her peace transcends the limits of time and space and stems from God's grace.

Christian faith is a continuing trek for Michelle. She is continually more convinced of the truth that is God and Christ, but her disdain for doctrine creates challenges for many churches. Like Jacob, she continues her struggle with God and with church hierarchy. This is how she summarized her understandings at the end of our conversation:

> I also see faith as a journey. I know my understanding of God has changed drastically from the beginning of my life until now. I hope it will continue to change because God is so overwhelmingly more than anything my brain can contain. I hope I am continuing to discover new things about God all the time. Everything I discover about God from day-to-day and through the years of my life has been better and better. I really struggle with the doctrine. I really struggle with church teachings, because they are limited in time, in space, and in context. I struggle a lot with Scripture because of the context and time limits placed on it. As I grow older, I am less willing to say things about God that . . . I would not blame on my worst enemy. For God to be

> vengeful, hateful, and arbitrary, I don't believe it. I don't want to say it, because to me that's heresy.

Michelle and I shared this conversation in 2010. Two years later, she sent me an e-mail update about her continuing sojourns:

> The journey continues. In December, my husband moved out, and after twenty-eight years of marriage, we are getting divorced. I've been interim pastor at [a mainline congregation] for a little over a year, thoroughly enjoying the challenge of "walking with" a little congregation on the edge of death, but perhaps coming back to life now after much hard work. I'll be looking for a new position now, full-time, as I have to support myself and will need health and retirement. Still questioning everything—with joy!

Michelle fits into Jamieson's definition of an Integrated Wayfinder and shows a Fowler Stage 5 Conjunctive Faith. She works within a "second naïveté" of paradox as she faces transitions in her life. Based on our conversations and the changing tapestry of her life, she will likely continue to change and struggle with God as Jacob did.

—For Reflection—

1. How do we try to make sense of God, life, and our challenges?
2. Read the account of Jacob wrestling with God in Genesis 32:22–31. When have you wrestled with God?
3. Jacob limped after he wrestled with God. What scars and limps do you show from your wrestling? Are they wounds or marks of grace?

18

Julian of Norwich

JULIAN OF NORWICH LIVED from approximately 1342 to 1416 in a time of great suffering, the Black Death, and the Hundred Years War between France and England. She became an anchoress, or hermit, in the Church of St. Julian, Norwich, England, in her early twenties, lived apart from the world in an apartment attached to the church, and engaged in prayer and spiritual counsel for the community. A window toward the church allowed her to participate in the services, and another window to the outside allowed her to interact with the outside community.

Julian asked God for three gifts that many people would avoid: an understanding of Christ's death and resurrection, a major physical illness, and three wounds, or stigmata. She believed this gift combination would enable her to identify with Christ and understand his love. She almost died from an illness at age thirty and subsequently began experiencing a series of visions of Jesus Christ as recorded in her book *Showings,* also titled *The Revelation of Divine Love*. Written shortly after her recovery, Julian provided a more extensive view of her visions approximately twenty years later in a longer version of *Showings*.

Julian embraced her faith journey and realized she saw God only dimly through her own abilities. God showed himself as he wished because "we can never seek God until the time when he in his goodness shows himself to us."[1] However, when we are in the wilderness times, beset with uncertainty, and surrounded with danger, God is there. In

1. Julian, *Showings*, 193.

one of her visions, not drowning even when we are deep under the water was a metaphor for God's limitless providence:

> Once my understanding was let down into the bottom of the sea, and there I saw green hills and valleys, with the appearance of moss strewn with seaweed and gravel. Then I understood in this way: that if a man or woman were there under the wide waters, if he could see God, as God is continually with man, he would be safe in soul and body, and come to no harm. And furthermore, he would have more consolation and strength than all this world can tell. For it is God's will that we believe that we see him continually, though it seems to us that the sight be only partial; and through this belief he makes us always to gain more grace, for God wishes to be seen, and he wishes to be sought, and he wishes to be expected, and he wishes to be trusted.[2]

God's unbounded love for even the most insignificant things expressed his unfathomable goodness. Julian wrote,

> And in this He showed me something small, no bigger than a hazelnut, lying in the palm of my hand, as it seemed to me, and it was as round as a ball. I looked at it with the eye of my understanding and thought: What can this be? I was amazed that it could last, for I thought that because of its littleness it would suddenly have fallen into nothing. And I was answered in my understanding: It lasts and always will, because God loves it; and thus everything has being through the love of God.[3]

Julian explored the union of the soul with God as a re-creation of the community that existed between the Father, Son, and Holy Spirit before time began. The following passage encapsulates much of her understanding that believers seek union with God and experience the holiness that comes from their increasing closeness. "And all this notwithstanding, we can never come to the full knowledge of God until we first clearly know our own soul. For until the time that it is in its full powers, we cannot be all holy; and that is when our sensuality by the power of Christ's Passion can be brought up into the substance, with all the profits of our tribulation which our Lord will make us obtain through mercy and grace."[4]

2. Ibid., 193–194.
3. Ibid., 183.
4. Ibid., 289.

Julian believed that people could know God only if he led them into knowledge that was beyond all understanding. Baby boomers and other searchers resemble Julian, embarking on a journey not knowing the ultimate destination. People on such a journey try to examine themselves and ultimately learn to know and love themselves. The strength for that knowledge and love only comes from God.

—For Reflection—

1. Do we deeply love the insignificant things, like Julian, because God loves them?
2. Do we dismiss them as irrelevant because they are not important to us?
3. Read Luke 12:27–31. What about the people we see every day and ignore because they are homeless, unemployed, have menial jobs, or otherwise don't affect us?

19

Teresa of Ávila

Teresa of Ávila (1515–1582) was born in the province of Ávila, Spain. Her grandfather was a *converso*, a Jew forced to convert to Christianity by the Spanish Inquisition. Her mother Beatriz died young, and Teresa's older sister stepped into the role of mother. Her father taught Teresa and her sisters how to read and write at home, since public education did not extend to women. When she was seven, Teresa and one of her brothers tried to run away and emulate the accounts of martyrs contained in books they read. An uncle found them at the edge of town and returned them home. Teresa commented, "Our greatest difficulty seemed to be our father and mother."[1]

When Teresa was sixteen, her sister married, and Teresa entered an Augustinian convent school. She remained a year and a half with the Augustinian nuns and experienced a religious call on her life, which she initially resisted, falling ill from the internal conflicts. After she recovered two years later, she entered the Carmelite convent near Ávila. She was an observant nun at first, although she was not particularly spiritual and rarely prayed. Less than two years later, she suffered paralyzed legs that kept her bedridden for three years. Prayer miraculously healed her.[2]

In about 1556, she had visions of Jesus Christ that continued for approximately two years. The nuns speculated that her visions were from the devil, and Teresa began to believe their suspicions and turned

1 Teresa, *Life*, 4.

2. Ibid., xxix–xxxi.

on herself ignoring the visions to avoid any such possibility. Her confessor, Francis de Borja, convinced her that the visions were authentic, and Teresa experienced them frequently when she allowed them to flood her life. "I felt I could maintain against all the world that my prayer was the work of God."[3]

Teresa's *The Interior Castle* viewed the journey to God as a series of seven concentric circles, with God at the center. The spiritual life was an inward journey moving from the body, through the senses, and into prayer. The inner levels involved deepening levels of prayer, and she drew on her experiences during her illnesses and visions. The first step was the "recollection prayer," leading to a "prayer of quiet," and then to a "prayer of union" (Teresa, *Interior Castle* 4–5). The prayer of union was a rapture-like ecstasy of becoming "one" with Jesus Christ. She wrote, "God places the soul in His own mansion which is in the very centre of the soul itself" (7.2.12). Teresa described the rapture of the union: "On returning to itself, the mind can recall what has been seen but is unable to describe it" (3.4.9).

Teresa invoked remembrances of the Hebrew people's travel through the wilderness. The journey toward union with God contained hints and signposts along the way that remind travelers of the benefits of the journey. She wrote, "Those children of Israel who were sent on first to the Land of Promise brought back tokens from it; so here our Lord seems to seek to show the soul something of the land to which it is travelling, to give it courage to pass through the trials of its painful journey, now that it knows where it must go to find rest" (6.5.11).

Christ was Teresa's center: "Let us first turn our thoughts to His prayer in the garden, then allow them to continue the subject until they reach the crucifixion" (6.7.13). Her union with God occurred within a strong Trinitarian structure: "All the Three Persons here communicate Themselves to the soul, speak to it and make it understand the words of our Lord in the Gospel that He and the Father and the Holy Ghost will come and make their abode with the soul which loves Him and keeps His commandments" (7.1.9).

Teresa's comments demonstrate her visions were not about an amorphous spirituality path, but rather they pointed to a faith journey within a Trinitarian framework. She believed strictly intellectual knowledge of God in a propositional nature was not what God desired.

3. Ibid., 216.

Rather, God desired the oneness and union that stems from a very close relationship (5.1.7). She believed God was there throughout her faith journey and had never abandoned her even when she did not sense his presence. This oneness and union points the way for baby boomers and others passing through Stages of Faith to take heart that the journey is beneficial even when it appears totally dark, dreary, and filled with disease and strife.

—For Reflection—

1. Do we embrace the movement though dark places?
2. Is Christ with us in the dark places?
3. Do we avoid pain whenever possible?

Story: Jim Trout

We worship an indescribable God. We write, paint, sing, shout, preach, talk, love, work, and perform innumerable other actions tying to describe God. Each of them captures at least some semblance of an attribute of God. Failure is inevitable, and desirable, because we cannot describe God fully or even mostly in human terms. Metaphors using all our senses are apparently the closest we can humanly come to describing God. Ezekiel struggled to write down his vision of heaven using the images of wheels inside wheels and the sounds of rushing waters (Ezek 1). Job finally realized that neither he nor his friends could even describe a small part of God. "I am unworthy—how can I reply to you? I put my hand over my mouth" (Job 40:4).

Jim Trout is familiar with Job-like experiences in his life. The youngest of nine children, he grew up in a traditional Catholic family. His family attended Mass frequently, and he served as an altar boy in his parish. Life was very placid for Jim until he was sixteen, when his father suddenly died. His father was an attorney, and his mother did not work outside the home so the family income stream ceased. They moved from a suburban style home into a cramped apartment and experienced a much lower standard of living.

His father's death had a profound influence on Jim's faith journey. Up to that point, he had not thought very much about the larger questions of life. He descended into despair and pondered the ways in which life's opportunities vanish so rapidly. The funeral pointed to a different reality when he saw God take tragedy and turn it into a triumph. Jim talks about his memories of the service:

> I remember my brothers and me bearing his coffin out of the church at the end of the funeral. This isn't TV, this isn't make believe. The weight of this casket is my father's body. This isn't pretend, this isn't a high school play that will be over. I remember putting the casket in the back of the hearse. At that moment, I felt like this is the coldest, darkest day of my life. I turned towards the church knowing that my mom was about to come

> out, just dreading this moment. I knew she'd just be crying and upset. The doors opened up and she came out. She was smiling. All of a sudden, the sky felt blue, sunny, and warm. She just looked up to the sky and said, "Thank you God for Jesus!"
>
> All of my dad's suffering was over. He had gone on to eternal life. It was her faith at that moment that I saw so vividly. It was just glowing. That moment God cemented himself right in the front of my brain for the rest of my life. I witnessed her taking a horrible situation in life and reversing it by shining the right light on it.

Jim and his family started attending what he describes as "Bible based churches." Several of them were deeply Pentecostal-influenced, and he saw people speaking in tongues and slain in the spirit who "scared the crap out of me." He describes one pastor who believed that the earth was the center of the universe. The stars were actually peepholes that God used to watch people on earth. He quickly discovered that the teachings in one church might be completely opposed to those in another church. The differences did not make sense to him; surprisingly he did not walk away from faith in disgust. He says, "I always had an interest and a thirst to find some answers."

Because of the timing of his father's death, Jim did not qualify for college financial aid after graduating from high school. He entered the Coast Guard prior to attending college. His next step along his ramble through faith came during Coast Guard basic training:

> One of the first moments when I really felt the strength of God was when I was at a breaking point in basic training. . . . All of a sudden, I was calmed and I felt a maturity. I felt a confidence, a release of my anxieties and my fears; I was in God's hands. I was being watched and being cared for but I wasn't alone. It just hit me, "What am I getting so upset about?" I'm being taken care of here. That was probably the first time I truly felt God's presence in my life.

Later in his Coast Guard service, he experienced major faith challenges, but the memory of this encounter sustained him. "I was struggling with my religion, struggling with my belief in God and Jesus Christ. . . . Now it's not as much of an issue because . . . I've matured."

One of Jim's sisters received a devastating cancer diagnosis when she was a senior in high school. She was "in and out of remission" for approximately fifteen years, and she finally passed away at the age of thirty-two. He remembers her as a person who always sought the fullness of life, and that perspective gives him wisdom in looking at death and tragedy. Like Job, he realized none of his actions could change the outcome for his sister.

Recently one of Jim's neighbors prayed for healing in the life of a family member who had a terminal illness. After the family member died, Jim recounts her reaction: "She now questions if there is a God. How could God be so mean to take him?" Jim comments, "[What] I'm praying for is that the person who is ill has found God. . . . [I pray that the person] has faith in God and has accepted Jesus Christ."

Jim reflects themes found in Ezekiel and in medieval mystics like Julian of Norwich or John of the Cross. He shows remarkable insight into ways of seeing and experiencing God:

> Sometimes I don't try to perceive God in anything that I can actually perceive. In other words, I don't try to fit God into any form, color, shape, or size. I see God as a source of power, strength, and enlightenment. . . . [He] has a love that is for everyone, a grace for everyone and offers a life for everyone who accepts his son who he sent to us. I can't even imagine entirely what God is. [He is] beyond my comprehension. I don't see how I could set a limit on his being. Description can often set limits.

About a year ago, Jim moved into a neighboring community. He and his wife decided that since their daughters moved away, they need a smaller home. The move has helped them financially, and this transition continued the theme of faith voyages in his life. Because of his life experiences and encounters, Jim underwent major faith transitions earlier than most people do, and is likely a Fowler Stage 4 or Stage 5 individual, either a Jamieson Transitional Explorer or Integrated Wayfinder. Like Ezekiel or Job, he recognizes that he cannot describe God and has learned to accept God as limitless.

—For Reflection—

1. When do we try to limit God by our own descriptions?
2. How much do our concepts limit him in our mind?
3. Read Job 40–41. How would you describe God in light of those chapters?

20

John of the Cross

John of the Cross lived from 1542 to 1591. Born on a high plateau in the Castile region of Spain to a textile merchant's son and a weaver's daughter, his father died shortly after John was born, which left the family destitute. John's mother placed him in a church orphanage school at Medina Del Campo since she could not feed him. He entered the Carmelite order in 1563, apparently fulfilling a life-long desire.

John's life and Teresa of Ávila's life intersected when Teresa met him in 1567, soon after she joined the convent at Medina del Campo. He came close to resigning the Carmelite Order because of the corruption and lax living he observed. However, Teresa persuaded him to remain in the Carmelite order and assist her with reform efforts. The reforms were controversial and, as a result, other Carmelites kidnapped John in 1577 and imprisoned him in a Toledo monastery.

John's very dark cell measured only six feet by ten feet. The monks beat him frequently in an attempt to force him to repudiate his reform efforts. After two months, he moved to a slightly better cell with a very small slit for light and air. There he began composing many of his works mentally because his jailers did not allow writing paper in the early stages of his imprisonment. While jailed, he composed *The Spiritual Canticle*, a commentary and re-working of the biblical Song of Solomon. After nine months, John escaped the cell. There are varying accounts of how he escaped. Some believed it was a miracle. Others said friends assisted his escape. Another account reported that he slowly unscrewed the lock and hinges on his door. He took his writings, climbed out a window using a rope made from his bedding, and left for areas more hospitable to his reform efforts.

John's major poem "The Dark Night" was an account of finding union with God through the journey of a night escape, the amazing wonders along the way, and communion with the beloved (God) during the night at the end of the journey.[1] John weaves a metaphor of God as a caring mother, who gives birth to a child, nurses it, carries it, and then must wean it to allow the child continued growth. God teaches the child to crawl, walk, talk, and leave childhood ways behind as it grows and morphs through Fowler's Stages of Faith.

The Ascent of Mount Carmel was his prose commentary on the poem "The Dark Night." For John "night" (*noche*) meant a positive time of purgation or purification rather than a negative time of dangers. He commented, "The soul journeys in darkness as though by night" (John of the Cross, *Ascent* 1.1.1). The transit toward God occurred in sequential stages, like the metaphor of multiple nights. The first night was "the lot of beginners, at the time God commences to introduce them into the state of contemplation" (1.1.2). The second night took place "in those who are already proficient, at the time God desires to lead them into the state of divine union. This purgation, of course, is more obscure, dark, and dreadful" (1.1.3). As we search and become closer to God, we depend less on ourselves and somewhat grudgingly become a passive participant letting God completely take the lead.

John clarified his reasons for using night as a metaphor for the wilderness trek toward God:

> We can offer three reasons for calling this journey toward union with God a night. The first has to do with the point of departure, because the individual must deprive himself of his appetite for worldly possessions. This denial and privation is like a night for all his senses. The second reason refers to the means or road along which a person travels to this union. Now this road is faith, and for the intellect, faith is also like a dark night. The third reason pertains to the point of arrival, namely, God. And God is also a dark night to man in this life. These three nights pass through a soul, or better, the soul passes through them in order to reach divine union with God. (1.2.1)

1. All quotations of the writings of John of the Cross, *The Ascent of Mount Carmel*, "The Dark Night," and *The Dark Night of the Soul* are from John of the Cross, *Collected Works*.

This text reflected a medieval understanding of a person being composed of the dichotomies of sense and spirit, or active and passive. A person interacts with the outside world through the senses of taste, sound, touch, smell, and sight. During the nights in the first phase, the senses undergo deprivation and are no longer guides to reality. Spirit, or the inner understanding of faith, memory, and direction, becomes the guide. When the intellect fails in the night, only faith remains as a direction. The purification of these is more difficult and painful than the elimination of the senses.

The next phase involves the movement from the active to the passive. The first two nights are active, and the person participates in his own purification by self-denial and faith in God. The following night is passive, in which God works by his own purifying touch. The terror in the passive experiences and purifications comes from the utter lack of personal control. The path is fully in the hand of God, operating on his own schedule.

John described, "Three different kinds of places, I find, by which God usually moves the will" (3.42.1). The first place was a "beautiful site" in which people "wander around looking for delight and gratification" (3.42.1). In the second place, God "moves the will to devotion" (3.42.2). The third place was one in which "God chooses to be invoked and worshipped" (3.42.5). John cited the examples of Mount Sinai (Gen 22:2, Exod 24:12) and Mount Horeb (1 Kings 19), high places in the midst of desolation. He comments, "God alone knows why he chooses one place in which to receive praise more than another" (*Ascent* 3.42.6).

John illustrated the ascent with a diagram (figures 2 and 3) as an aid to understanding the poem and the possible paths up the mountain. The side paths are the "ways of the imperfect spirit" by pursuits such as "goods of heaven," "joy," "knowledge," "consolation," and "rest." Although they appear to lead to the summit, those routes lead back down off the mountain. The path that leads to the top (The Perfect Spirit) is labeled *nada*, *nada*, *nada*, Spanish for "nothing, nothing, nothing." We bring nothing to the journey; Christ is the leader and sole signpost leading with the pillar of fire by night. The further we move along Fowler's Stages of Faith, the more we abandon the "ways of the imperfect spirit" and embrace the center path.

Sketch of Mount Carmel by St. John of the Cross.

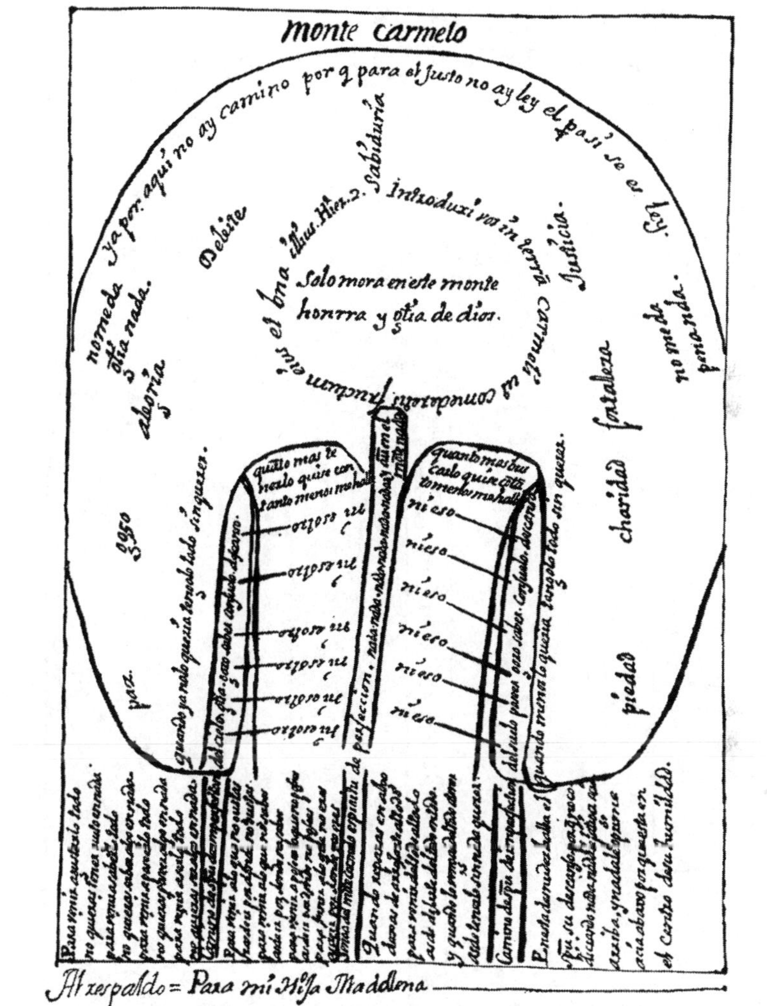

Figure 3. John's Original Drawing in ***The Ascent of Mt. Carmel.***[2]

2. John of the Cross, *Collected Works*, 110.

English translation of terms used in St. John's original drawing.

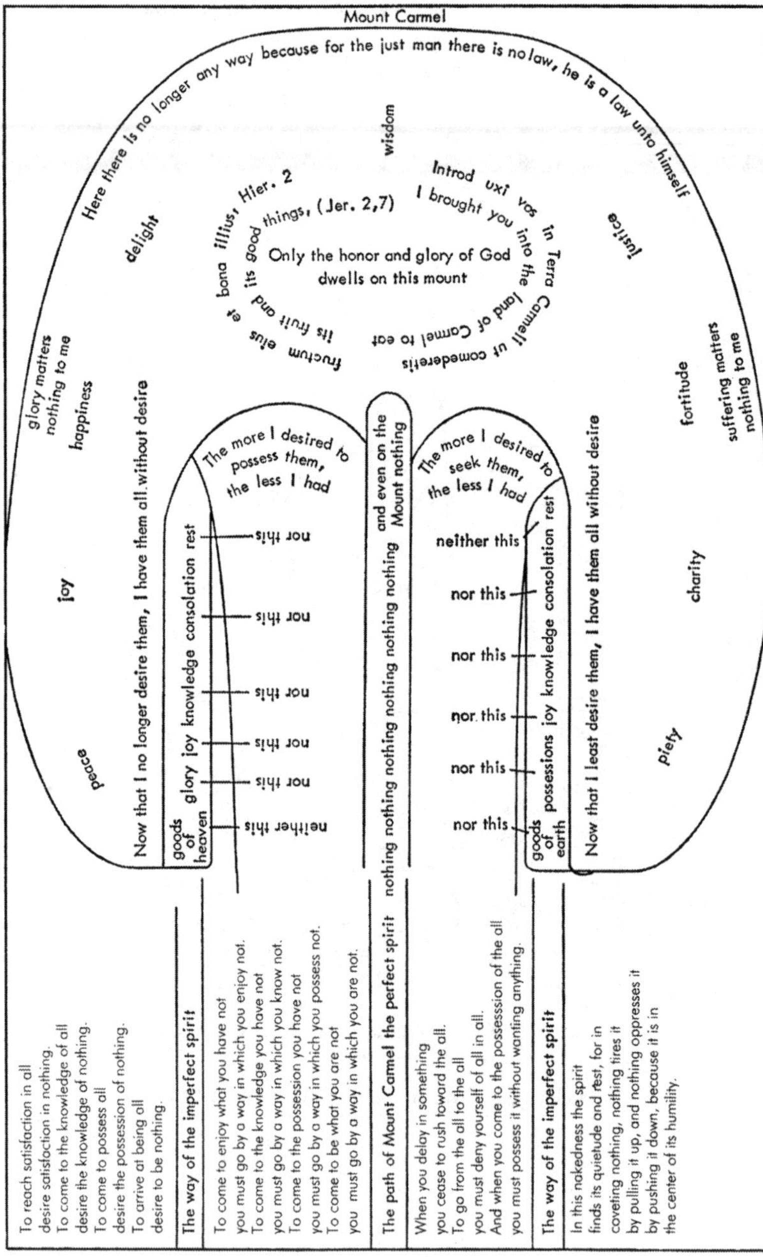

Figure 4. English Translation of John's Drawing.[3]

3. Ibid., 111.

John referred to the darkness as *la noche oscura*, the dark night of the soul, as a time that was unknown and mysterious. This darkness, however, was not evil or a force of evil like that found in *la noche tinieblas*, a night of trouble or evil. Rather, John described a time in which the rest of the world was obscure and the soul focused on the truly important factors. John experienced vision and clarity in this darkness and explained, "This dark night is an inflow of God into the soul, which purges it of its habitual ignorances and imperfections, natural and spiritual, and which the contemplatives call infused contemplation or mystical theology" (2.5.1).

The dark time contained two distinct parts: the dark night of the senses and the dark night of the spirit. In the dark night of the senses, or an "active" darkness, the senses underwent an emptying process. John wrote, "The necessity to pass through this dark night . . . to attain divine union with God arises from the fact that all of a person's attachments to creatures are pure darkness in God's sight" (1.4.1). During this time, the person was an active participant who decided to journey toward the emptying. The darkness focused attention on the distractions of "light" that could be jettisoned in a period resembling dusk.

The dark night of the spirit, a "passive" time, was similar to midnight, a time of *nada*, or nothing. The wayfarer can no longer do anything. In this experience, God freed people from the idols they made of possessions, relationships, feelings, and behavior during this passive time. "The passive way is that in which one does nothing, but God accomplishes the work in the soul while the soul acts as the recipient" (1.13.1).

John continued the explanation of "The Dark Night" in another prose work, *The Dark Night of the Soul.* It examined the passive part of the night in more detail: "The first purgation or night is bitter and terrible to the senses. But nothing can be compared to the second, for it is horrible and frightful to the spirit" (*The Dark Night of the Soul*, 1.8.2).

John maps explorations of unplanned discovery that can sometimes be extremely painful. Others experience times of peace in turning over all responsibility to God. All of these are excursions of liberation, initiated by recognition that life has become meaningless or tastes bitter. He emphasizes that faith transformations can last many years, and those who travel may not realize they were on a journey until they reach its later phases. "In the obscurity of the night, we may not recognize that imprint or the presence that makes it. But as we become freer, we have more glimpsed of the dawn, more awareness of these deeper currents of our lives."[4] David captures the unexpected transparency of the darkness in one of his Psalms of lament:

> If I say, "Surely the darkness will hide me
> and the light become night around me,"
> even the darkness will not be dark to you;
> the night will shine like the day,
> for darkness is as light to you. (Ps 139:11–12)

—For Reflection—

1. When have you needed John's hope that we are not alone?
2. When were you lost in the darkness or enduring painful transitions?
3. Have you seen God's face in the darkness?

4. May, *Dark Night*, 96.

Story: Mary Dobson

Sometimes I think of the comedy and tragedy masks that represent the theater. One actor can take on two opposite personas in the same performance. Life imitates art when it is not clear if a life challenge is a blessing or a curse. Sometimes the difference is minimal or nonexistent. Psalm 102 captures the dichotomy:

> In the course of my life he broke my strength;
> he cut short my days.
> So I said:
> "Do not take me away, O my God, in the midst of my days;
> your years go on through all generations. (Ps 102:23–24)

Is this passage a lament or a praise? Can it be both?

Mary Dobson grew up in a small Southern town with two supportive parents. She comments, "Growing up and going to church every Sunday was something that was expected. You know there is a God. You learn the Bible verses and stories. There was belief but it was never tested as a child." After finishing high school, she moved to the west coast to continue her college education. Not long after graduating with a nursing degree, she married her first husband. They had two children together and she frequently took on the role of single parent when her husband was on lengthy sea deployments with the Navy.

A few years later, Mary received a devastating cancer diagnosis. "My son was three and a half and my daughter was thirteen months old. . . . You don't expect when you are twenty-five years old to be told suddenly you have twenty-four to thirty-six months to live. My bargain with God was 'let me see my children grow up,' not knowing if it was a realistic bargain. Then it became less of a bargain but an acceptance that 'it is what it is.' As I got worse, and got better, and got worse, and got better, and [I] survived. It was more of an acceptance than anything else."

Mary's health condition fluctuated wildly because of her husband, who was alcoholic, abusive, and unfaithful. Her cancer symptoms would almost vanish when he was at sea. When her husband was at home, she was rarely able to fight her way out of bed in the morning. "I ceased to be the person I was before I got married. . . . I didn't know it was okay to leave [my husband]. . . . He took away my self-esteem and made me question my self-worth. I became the typical codependent battered wife." Mary endured the pain and suffering for seventeen years before she divorced him. "I didn't know that leaving a marriage was an option because I wasn't brought up that way."

In the middle of the divorce pain, Mary's cancer symptoms returned. "I thought I had come out of remission, but I was diagnosed with another cancer." Her devastating diagnosis was myeloma blood cancer. The oncologist told her parents to "go home and make it a good year" since they did not expect Mary to survive the year. "It was probably the best year of my life and the one that my kids remember most." Her year walking through the "valley of the shadow of death" (Psalm 23.4) turned heartbreaking when Mary's mother died unexpectedly while at work. "It was a year that we would not have made all the memories, if I had not been sick. We thought we were making the memories for me, because I was the one dying. We were making memories for my family and my mother." Was this a year for the comedy mask or the tragedy mask?

Mary's cancers remained in remission until the early 2000s, when she developed cancerous tumors likely precipitated by heavy doses of chemotherapy and radiation. Her overwhelming health challenges caused Mary to re-evaluate her life and decide what she wanted to discard and what she needed to keep. She overcame her fear of repeated failure and ended a second marriage that she describes as "miserable." "I changed from worrying about what others thought and started concentrating on what made me happy. . . There's going to come a time when you don't get to go back to do the things you want to, because you have gotten older, or sicker, or the opportunities aren't there any longer."

Through these experiences, Mary's faith matured. This growing process occurred more rapidly because of her life-threatening and life-altering experiences. The progression started not long after her first cancer diagnosis. "I wasn't sure I could do this. I couldn't handle it, yet the peace washed over me and told me that I would and I could. I had to hand it over [to God]."

Her journey persisted with many detours and unexpected turns. Recently she has come to a new place of acceptance solidly in Fowler's Stage 5 and Jamieson's Integrated Wayfinder. She no longer even tries to choose between tragedy or comedy mask since both are the same at their root. Pain and joy are the same for Mary; she cannot tell the difference any more. "I'm not afraid to die. I prefer to go later rather than sooner. You dwell on it when you first get sick and then you put it away in the back of your mind. Then you tend to drag it out and deal with it. . . I see people who are scared to die. I think the only reason they are scared to die is because they don't know the love of Christ. . . The sorrow is not on our side. The sorrow will be for those left alive."

—For Reflection—

1. Read 2 Corinthians 12:7–10. How does Paul's "thorn in my flesh" resemble the two masks?
2. Can we really see a difference between tragedy and comedy in our lives?
3. Do both masks merge in Christ?

21

Where Do We Go Next?

For too many of us, we are confronted with a church of our own making, one that has misplaced the basic understanding of what it means to be a follower of Christ, with what it means to be a business. We have developed unmotivated people sitting in our pews who expect the "paid staff" to do all the work. We have developed a system where members of different churches do not speak to each other, or connect in any way, because "they don't think like us." We have a system that encourages just a few to do all the work, and burn out. We have developed into a people who do not think for ourselves, we have become followers of our pastors and not of Christ.

—John O'Keefe,
"Leadershift in the Church," www.johncokeefe.com

This is a book about faith and hope in stories. The stories take shape in the faith journeys of people, taking on sinews, bones, and flesh when they intersect with God and life. When we are in the trackless wilderness thinking everyone has abandoned us, perhaps these stories will give you the hope you desperately desire.

As we have seen throughout these pages, faith journeys are not a new or postmodern phenomenon. The witness of Christian scripture with its prominence of travel shows how Christ connects with the wayfaring stranger. Extensive Judeo-Christian experience affirms the validity of voyage and wilderness times. The desert fathers and mothers sought solace and loneliness so they could focus on the trek with God. The medieval mystics delved deeply into themselves and into God, finding profound insights where they least expected them. The baby boomer stories throughout the book show how God connects with us during those times, even when we do not recognize his presence.

Connecting with Baby Boomers

Baby boomers are the cusp generation that marks the division between the enlightenment and the postmodern eras. Daniel Pink refers to them when he observes, "When the cold front of demographics meets the warm front of unrealized dreams, the result will be a thunderstorm of purpose the likes of which the world has never seen."[1] He envisions a tripod of motivational factors: *autonomy*, *mastery*, and *purpose*. *Autonomy* is the recognition that people are valued individuals of a community, and thrive when treated accordingly. Pink defines *mastery* as a desire for constant improvement in things that matter. His term mastery would equate to discipleship growth in a Christian context. *Purpose* is a desire to be part of a group or a cause that transcends each of us as an individual.

Autonomy

Fowler's Stages of Faith and Jamieson's Church Leaver studies illustrate how people desire increasing autonomy as they move through the faith stage hierarchy. God wired us to be inquisitive and self-directed. We want to explore and experiment. The semi-cliché rationale that drives human exploration—"Because it's there"—is a seed planted deep within us by God. Adam and Eve ate the forbidden fruit (Gen 3). Moses went over to see the flames that did not burn up the bush (Exod 3:3). Samuel did not ignore God's voice but instead asked Eli if he was the one speaking (1 Sam 3). In John, Jesus said to the two men following him, "'Come,' he replied, 'and you will see'" (John 1:39).

This autonomy not an increasing rugged self-reliant individualism but rather an increasing interdependence while still "acting with

1. Pink, *Drive*, Kindle e-book, location 1781.

choice."[2] Some baby boomers have unsuccessfully attempted to self-direct their lives, suffering the "slings and arrows of outrageous fortune," as Shakespeare summarized in *Hamlet*. Autonomy is not the false hope of the management buzzword "empowerment." Rather autonomy builds community because each member is valued for his or her inherent worth stemming from God. Did Jesus empower Peter when he said, "On this rock I will build my church" (Matt 16:18)? He gave Peter the autonomy to act independently while still being a fully devoted follower of Christ. Empowerment suggests an instantaneous "fix" while autonomy suggests a learned self-motivated path while still interdependent with Christ and the community. Peter devoted his life to following Christ. His stumbles along the way give us hope when we realize the freedom Christ entrusts us with makes us increasingly dedicated followers of Christ.

Mastery

Mastery is a desire for constant improvement in things that matter. Another definition is discipleship growth in a Christian context, applying to baby boomers, or any other generation. Does this mastery come from attending classes, more Bible reading, or maybe from joining small groups? Unfortunately, the results fall short most of the time. The Willow Creek *Reveal* study cited in chapter 1 conveys the sad truth about most discipleship programs—they are dismal failures.

I am not sure intensive Bible study leads to mastery. Bible study leads to becoming an expert in Bible trivia, but *by itself*, intensive Bible research does not lead to a deeper understanding of how God speaks to us. None of the baby boomers stories contained in this book show breakthroughs *solely* from reading the Bible.

Maybe a better approach is to couple mastery with purpose, and let mastery follow purpose. The motivation of purpose leads to seeking mastery. Imagine Jamieson's metaphor of the swim team member who finds the joy of exploration into uncharted waters with a small group of compatriots. We who are looking into unfamiliar waters still practice swimming and become more skilled. We also exercise our exploration skills to discover new and uncharted areas.

2. Pink, *Drive*, Kindle e-book, location 1148.

Mastery flowing from purpose matches up with the Stages of Faith framework. We increase in our inquiries and appreciation of other viewpoints, recognizing that the undergirding of our appreciation of other viewpoints originates from a solid understanding of our own core faith and beliefs. We also begin to appreciate the amalgam of service and study, the Bible and practice, the community small and large, the melding of similar yet paradoxical concepts.

Purpose

Daniel Pink captures much of essential human motivation by viewing it from a self-determined framework. The major adjustment needed is shifting the source of motivating drive from inherent human nature to a God inspired source. Treating the individual as valuable and unique allows people to flourish. When churches revalue baby boomers and others, lifting them up as Jesus did, amazing results occur: "There was a woman present, so twisted and bent over with arthritis that she couldn't even look up. She had been afflicted with this for eighteen years. When Jesus saw her, he called her over. 'Woman, you're free!' He laid hands on her and suddenly she was standing straight and tall, giving glory to God" (Luke 13:11–13 MSG).

We are seeing a renewed sense of purpose, or at least the pursuit of purpose, in society today. Most people sense that we will not see dramatically increasing personal wealth in the west during the decades ahead. The entire philosophical, meaning, and economic framework of the world is undergoing a major transformation currently. Purpose is moving to the forefront as the dominant factor.

People, and especially baby boomers, seek purpose and want something to believe in. They want a metaphor that gives their life meaning so when they glimpse the finite end of their own life while simultaneously looking backward, they can say, "My life was worth the effort." They want to have a purpose like Paul, "I consider everything a loss compared to the surpassing greatness of knowing Christ Jesus my Lord, for whose sake I have lost all things. I consider them rubbish, that I may gain Christ and be found in him" (Phil 3:8–9).

Searching for Community

People of any generation seek a sense of purpose, and individuals move through different Stages of Faith as they undergo life changes. Baby boomers may have undergone more stages because of their life spans and the major societal shifts in their lifetimes. In 2006 baby boomers started turning sixty, asking themselves, "Where did the time go?" Looking back through the years and passages, we can see the stages and transitions more clearly. Churches focused on a single stage of faith cannot create a sense of community that comes from valuing all people. Some of those organizations become inward looking, focusing on worship, children's ministry, or other pursuits and minimize showing the love of Christ to the world. Baby boomers, especially, will leave and look elsewhere if they cannot find an outlet for their God-inspired purpose through church affiliation.

Many current churches resemble secular businesses with a CEO (lead pastor), paid staff (pastors and directors), hierarchical control (administrative board and staff hierarchy), and high overhead expenses (pastoral salaries and rent/mortgage). In *Boneyard*, John O'Keefe refers to these organizations as *industrial churches* since they modeled their structure as an industrial revolution corporation. O'Keefe believes this type of church develops leaders and seeks numerical growth at the expense of growing disciples.[3] Unfortunately, such organizations frequently treat baby boomers and others as immature caterpillars when some are in a chrysalis stage ready to emerge, and some are butterflies "moving quickly and easily between many Christian groups."[4]

Can churches that focus on caterpillars learn to welcome people on faith journeys? Such change is challenging, and those churches that cannot change may not have a long lifetime ahead of them. Jamieson writes, "Too often church leaders suspect the way to keep dissatisfied people happy is to give them a role in leadership or a significant leadership position within a specific aspect of the church."[5] This approach is rarely successful because the people are frequently at a different faith stage than the church expects. Usually the top leaders expect support of existing organizational goals when new people join a church's leadership

3. O'Keefe, *Boneyard*, 13–15.
4. Jamieson, *Chrysalis*, 107.
5. Jamieson, *A Churchless Faith*, 129.

team. Fowler's Stage 3 individuals look to defined congregational leaders for their authority. Stage 4 people value individualism. Stage 5 re-integrates individualism with the paradox of simultaneous submission to church leaders. If the focus of the goals is Stage 3 without room for Stage 4 or Stage 5 populaces, then a Christian growing into those stages quickly realizes the futility of attempting change in the church. They do not want to be a caterpillar again.

The literal meaning of *ekklesia*, the Greek word for church, is "called out" consisting of the preposition *ek* (out of) and the verb *kaleo* (to call).[6] In the Greek context, it is an ordinary word referring to a gathering of people without religious significance. This definition suggests churches are the people of God who meet as communities without pretense and with minimal organization. Eugene Peterson describes his vision of the true nature of church, "All I am insisting is that if we want to embrace a truly Spirit-formed church, we must embrace the messy conditions—the complexity of relationships both interpersonal and Trinitarian, the many levels of maturity and immaturity, the ever-present vulnerability of everyone to sin—out of which the Holy Spirit is working. If we are serious about church and want to participate in what the Holy Spirit is doing, these are the conditions. Get used to it."[7]

What You Can Do Next

Take time to probe into your own history more deeply. Each of us are on a journey of discovery and each of has a unique story. Where have you come from? Where do you see your life going? Look back and recognize where Jesus journeyed alongside you in life and what that looked like.

I'm suggesting that you write down your faith journey—a narrative of the important events in your life and how God interacted with them. The questions at the end of each chapter are a good beginning. They will start you thinking about the tapestry of your life with its times of joy, times of sorrow, times of frustration, and the other times in your life.

Next, go a step further and examine the questions in the Appendix. All the stories in the book came from these interview questions.

6. Arndt, Danker, and Bauer, *Greek-English Lexicon*, 303–304.

7. Peterson, *Practice Resurrection*, Kindle e-book, locations 2540–2544.

They are not easy to answer, and some require deep thought. Plan a quiet retreat alone or with a friend and write out your responses.

Your journey narrative becomes an antidote to boredom, burnout, and frustration. The process of going through the questions and then writing the responses focuses you on the important aspects of your life situation. The less important aspects seem to vanish in the work of reflecting and writing. Aspects of your life that you need to change become much clearer. Minor aspects that you have been worried about become much less of a stumbling block. The memoir can be antidote for frustrations with the church. It provides a path to continue and remain engaged in church even when church constantly disappoints you. Alternately, it might lead to a redefining of church in your life.

Still after all my frustrations, my quests, my failings, and my doubts about the life expectancy of "church as we know it," I remain fully committed to Jesus Christ as the one and the only one whom we follow. The fallow time of the church in the west will lead to something better, on God's timing and not our timing. I invite you to join me on a voyage of discovery, engaging in *Good Faith Hunting* and seeking after the heart of God.

Appendix

Faith Development Interview Questions

THE STORIES THROUGHOUT THIS book come from interviews I conducted, modeled after James Fowler's Faith Development theory. These individual accounts demonstrate how each person's faith changed as he or she underwent life transitions, showing how Christian faith is a journey and not a constant climb toward holiness.

The feedback to questions asked sheds light on the interviewee's deep convictions and sources of meaning both independently as well as within a particular peer or influence group. The inquiries also illustrate faith as a journey since they focus on faith and life transitions, eliciting comments about painful and troubling times in each of their lives.

These are the questions used in the interviews:[1]

1. Could you please give me a brief biographical sketch of your life?
2. Reflecting on your life, identify the most important event. What other chapters and events stand out as especially important?
3. Are there past relationships that have been important to your development as a person?
4. Do you recall any changes in relationships that have had a significant impact on your life or your way of thinking about things?
5. How has your image of God and relation to God changed across your life's chapters? Who or what is God to you now?
6. Have you ever had moments of intense joy or breakthrough

1. The questions derive from the list in Fowler, Streib, and Keller, *Manual for Faith Development Research*, 17–21.

experiences that have affirmed or changed your sense of life's meaning?

7. Have you experienced times of crisis or suffering in your life, or times when you felt profound disillusionment or that life had no meaning? What happened to you at these times?
8. How have these experiences affected you?
9. How have your parents influenced you in the past? Has your relationship changed with them over the years? If so, what caused the change? How would you describe your current relationship?
10. Are there any other current relationships that seem important to you? This could include relationships with persons living or dead.
11. What groups, institutions, or causes, do you identify with? Why do you think that these are important to you?
12. What gives your life meaning?
13. If you could change one thing about yourself or your life, what would you most want to change?
14. Are there any beliefs, values, or commitments that seem important to your life right now?
15. When or where do you find yourself most in communion or harmony with God or the universe? Do you find yourself in conflict?
16. When you have an important decision to make, how do you generally go about making it? Can you give me an example? If you have a very difficult problem to solve, to whom or what would you look for guidance?
17. Do you think that actions can be right or wrong? If so, in your opinion, what makes an action right?
18. Are there certain actions or types of actions that are always right under any circumstances? Are there certain moral opinions that you think everyone should agree on?
19. Do you think that human life has a purpose? If so, what do you think it is? Is there a plan for our lives, or are we affected by a power or powers beyond our control?
20. What does death mean to you? What happens to us when we die?

21. Do you consider yourself a religious person? What does this mean to you? Would you rather describe yourself as spiritual? As a believer?
22. Are there any religious ideas, symbols, or rituals that are important to you, or have been important to you? If so, what are these and why are they important?
23. Do you pray, meditate, or perform any other spiritual discipline?
24. What is sin, to your understanding?
25. How do you explain the presence of evil in our world?

Bibliography

"Anne Rice Leaves Christianity." CNN Belief Blog. No pages. Online: http://religion.blogs.cnn.com/2010/07/30/anne-rice-leaves-christianity/.

Arndt, William, Frederick W. Danker, and Walter Bauer. *A Greek-English Lexicon of the New Testament and Other Early Christian Literature*. Chicago: University of Chicago, 2000.

Augustine, Saint. *Confessions*. Translated by Henry Chadwick. Oxford, UK: Oxford University Press, 1991.

Bailey, Sarah Pulliam. "Q & A: Anne Rice on Following Christ Without Christianity." Christianity Today. No pages. Online: http://www.christianitytoday.com/ct/2010/augustweb-only/43-21.0.html.

Barna, George. *The Second Coming of the Church*. Nashville, TN: Word, 1998.

———. *Revolution: Finding Vibrant Faith Beyond the Walls of the Church*. Carol Stream, IL: Tyndale House, 2005.

Bonaventure, John. "The Soul's Journey into God." In *Bonaventure: The Soul's Journey into God, The Tree of Life, The Life of St. Francis*. New York: Paulist Press, 1978. 51–116.

Bruce, F. F. *Paul: Apostle of the Heart Set Free*. Grand Rapids, MI: William B. Eeerdmans, 1977.

Brueggemann, Walter. *Texts Under Negotiation: The Bible and Postmodern Imagination*. Minneapolis: Fortress Press, 1993.

———. *The Psalms and the Life of Faith*. Minneapolis: Augsburg Fortress, 1995.

———. *Theology of the Old Testament: Testimony, Dispute, Advocacy*. Minneapolis: Fortress, 1997.

Soanes, Catherine, and Angus Stevenson, eds. *Concise Oxford English Dictionary*. Oxford, UK: Oxford University Press, 2004.

Cross, F. L., and Elizabeth A. Livingstone. *The Oxford Dictionary of the Christian Church*. 3rd rev. ed. Oxford, UK: Oxford University Press, 2005.

The Barna Group. "Do Americans Change Faiths?" No pages. Online: http://www.barna.org/faith-spirituality/412-do-americans-change-faiths.

Douthat, Ross. "Can Liberal Christianity Be Saved?" The New York Times. No pages. Online: http://www.nytimes.com/2012/07/15/opinion/douthat-can-liberal-christianity-be-saved.html.

Duin, Julia. *Quitting Church: Why the Faithful Are Fleeing and What to Do about It*. Grand Rapids, MI: Baker Books, 2008.

Fowler, James W. *Stages of Faith: The Psychology of Human Development and the Quest for Meaning*. San Francisco: HarperSanFrancisco, 1981.

———. *Becoming Adult, Becoming Christian: Adult Development and Christian Faith*. San Francisco: Harper & Row, 1984.

Fowler, James W., Heinz Streib, and Barbara Keller. *Manual for Faith Development Research*. 3rd ed. Atlanta, GA: Center for Research in Faith and Moral Development, 2004.

Hanson, Amy. *Baby Boomers and Beyond: Tapping the Ministry Talents and Passions of Adults Over 50*. San Francisco: Jossey-Bass, 2010.

Hawking, Greg L., and Cally Parkinson. *Reveal: Where Are You? The Answer Will Transform Your Church*. Barrington, IL: Willow Creek Association, 2007.

Holmes, Michael William. *The Apostolic Fathers: Greek Texts and English Translations*. Updated ed. Grand Rapids, MI: Baker Books, 1999.

Songfacts. "(I Can't Get No) Satisfaction by The Rolling Stones." No pages. Online: http://www.songfacts.com/detail.php?id=449.

Jamieson, Alan. *A Churchless Faith: Faith Journeys beyond the Churches*. London: SPCK, 2002.

———. *Chrysalis: The Hidden Transformation in the Journey of Faith*. Milton Keynes, UK: Paternoster, 2007.

John of the Cross, Saint. *Collected Works of Saint John of the Cross*. Translated by Kieran Kavanaugh and Otilio Rodriguez. Washington, DC: Institute of Carmelite Studies, 1991.

Julian of Norwich. *Showings*. Translated by Edmund Colledge and James Walsh. The Classics of Western Spirituality. Mahwah, NJ: Paulist Press, 1978.

Koehler, Ludwig, Walter Baumgartner, M.E.J Richardson, and Johann Jakob Stamm. *The Hebrew and Aramaic Lexicon of the Old Testament*. Electronic ed. Leiden, The Netherlands: E. J. Brill, 1999.

Kunhardt, Jessie. "Anne Rice: 'I Quit Being a Christian.'" The Huffington Post. No pages. Online: http://www.huffingtonpost.com/2010/07/29/anne-rice-i-quit-being-a_n_663915.html.

Lane, Belden C. *The Solace of Fierce Landscapes: Exploring Desert and Mountain Spirituality*. New York: Oxford University Press, 1998.

Centers for Disease Control and Prevention. *Live Births, Birth Rates, and Fertility Rates, by Race: United States, 1909-2003*. 2004. Online: http://www.cdc.gov/nchs/data/statab/natfinal2003.annvol_01.pdf.

Louth, Andrew. *The Wilderness of God*. Nashville, TN: Abingdon Press, 1997.

Lyotard, Jean-François. *The Postmodern Condition: A Report on Knowledge*. Translated by Geoff Bennington and Brian Massumi. Vol. 10 of Theory and History of Literature. Minneapolis, MN: University of Minnesota Press, 1984.

May, Gerald G. *The Dark Night of the Soul: A Psychiatrist Explores the Connection between Darkness and Spiritual Growth*. New York: HarperOne, 2003.

Martínez, Florentino García, and Eibert J. C. Tigchelaar, eds. *The Dead Sea Scrolls Study Edition*. Vol. 1. Leiden, The Netherlands: Brill, 1997.

Miles, Jack. "Religion Makes a Comeback. (Belief to Follow.)." *The New York Times Magazine*, 7 December 1997, 56–59.

Moore, Michael S. "Numbers." In *The Transforming Word: A One Volume Commentary on the Bible*. Edited by Mark W. Hamilton. Abiline: TX: Abiline Christian University Press, 2009. 185–202.

O'Keefe, John C. *Boneyard: Creatives Will Change the Way We Lead in the Church*. Sacramento, CA: DeadFish Publishing, 2010.

Parker, Simon B., ed. *Ugaritic Narrative Poetry*. Vol. 9. SBL Writings from the Ancient World. Atlanta, GA: Scholars Press, 1997.

Peterson, Eugene H. *Practice Resurrection: A Conversation on Growing Up in Christ*. Grand Rapids, MI: William B. Eerdmans, 2010.

Phillips, W. David, "The End of the James Finlayson Story. . . For Now, April 10, 2009." No pages. Online: http://www.wdavidphillips.com/the-end-of-the-james-finlayson-storyfor-now.

———. "The Story of James Finlayson, July 11, 2006." No pages. Online: http://www.wdavidphillips.com/the-story-of-james-finlayson.

Pink, Daniel H. *Drive: The Surprising Truth about What Motivates Us.* New York: Riverhead Books, 2009.

Polanyi, Michael. *Personal Knowledge: Towards a Post-Critical Philosophy.* Chicago: The University of Chicago Press, 1974.

Rice, Anne. "Important Information on Anne's Decision to Quit Christianity in the Name of Christ." No pages. Online: http://www.annerice.com/Chamber-Chistianity.html.

Roof, Wade Clark. *Spiritual Marketplace: Baby Boomers and the Remaking of American Religion.* Princeton, NJ: Princeton University Press, 1999.

United States Census Bureau. *Selected Characteristics of Baby Boomers 42 to 60 Years Old in 2006.* Online: http://www.census.gov/population/age/publications/files/2006babyboomers.pdf.

Sittser, Gerald L. *Water from a Deep Well: Christian Spirituality from Early Martyrs to Modern Missionaries.* Downers Grove, IL: IVP Books, 2007.

Stackhouse, Max L., and David W. Miller. "Economic Ethics." In *The Encyclopedia of Christianity.* Edited by Erwin Fahlbusch and Geoffrey William Bromiley, 2:12–23. Grand Rapids, MI: William B. Eerdmans, 2003.

Stewart, Henry. "The Messenger," *The United Methodist Reporter*, September 1999.

Stetzer, Ed. First-Person: SBC 2011 Statistical Realities." No pages. Online: http://www.bpnews.net/BPFirstPerson.asp?ID=38035.

Sweet, Leonard. *So Beautiful, Divine Designs for Life and the Church.* Colorado Springs, CO: David C. Cook, 2009.

———. *Viral: How Social Networking Is Poised to Ignite Revival.* New York: WaterBrook Multnomah, 2012.

Sweet, Leonard, and Frank Viola. *Jesus Manifesto: Restoring the Supremacy and Sovereignty of Jesus Christ.* New York: Thomas Nelson, 2010.

Taylor, Barbara Brown. *Leaving Church: A Memoir of Faith.* San Francisco: HarperSanFrancisco, 2006.

Teresa of Ávila, St. *The Life of Saint Teresa of Jesus of the Order of Our Lady of Carmel.* Translated by David Lewis. 3rd enl. ed. London: Thomas Baker, 1904.

———. *The Interior Castle or The Mansions.* Translated by The Benedictines of Stanbrook. 3rd ed. London: Thomas Baker, 1921.

Ward, Benedicta, trans. *The Sayings of the Desert Fathers: The Alphabetical Collection.* Rev. ed. Vol. 59 of Cistercian Studies Series. Trappist, KY: Cistercian Publications, 1984.

Gallup, Inc. "US Confidence in Organized Religion at Low Point." No pages. Online: http://www.gallup.com/poll/155690/Confidence-Organized-Religion-Low-Point.aspx.